# A HISTORY OF BRITISH ROYAL JUBILEES

*For my parents, Brian and Christina, and my husband and son,*
*Roger and Galahad.*

# A HISTORY OF BRITISH ROYAL JUBILEES

JUNE WOOLERTON

AN IMPRINT OF PEN & SWORD BOOKS LTD.
YORKSHIRE – PHILADELPHIA

First published in Great Britain in 2022 by
PEN AND SWORD HISTORY
An imprint of
Pen & Sword Books Ltd
Yorkshire – Philadelphia

Copyright © June Woolerton, 2022

ISBN 978 1 39906 276 3

The right of June Woolerton to be identified as Author of this work has been asserted by her in accordance with the Copyright, Designs and Patents Act 1988.

A CIP catalogue record for this book is available from the British Library.

All rights reserved. No part of this book may be reproduced or transmitted in any form or by any means, electronic or mechanical including photocopying, recording or by any information storage and retrieval system, without permission from the Publisher in writing.

Typeset in Times New Roman 12/16 by
SJmagic DESIGN SERVICES, India.
Printed and bound in the UK by CPI Group (UK) Ltd.

Pen & Sword Books Limited incorporates the imprints of Atlas, Archaeology, Aviation, Discovery, Family History, Fiction, History, Maritime, Military, Military Classics, Politics, Select, Transport, True Crime, Air World, Frontline Publishing, Leo Cooper, Remember When, Seaforth Publishing, The Praetorian Press, Wharncliffe Local History, Wharncliffe Transport, Wharncliffe True Crime and White Owl.

*For a complete list of Pen & Sword titles please contact*
PEN & SWORD BOOKS LIMITED
47 Church Street, Barnsley, South Yorkshire, S70 2AS, England
E-mail: enquiries@pen-and-sword.co.uk
Website: www.pen-and-sword.co.uk

Or
PEN AND SWORD BOOKS
1950 Lawrence Rd, Havertown, PA 19083, USA
E-mail: Uspen-and-sword@casematepublishers.com
Website: www.penandswordbooks.com

# Contents

# Chapter One

# The Origins of Jubilees

As the Golden Jubilee of Queen Victoria approached in 1887, a member of the Royal Historical Society in London decided that the general population needed some help in understanding why a huge party was about to overtake the country. Ahead of the big day, a collection of anecdotes from the Jubilee of the Queen's grandfather, George III, was put on sale, as an example of what to expect from the much hyped celebrations. It was a smart move; very few of those involved in the anniversary of Victoria's reign had ever lived through a Jubilee before and the concept of marking a monarch's reign with a nationwide party was still a strange one.

George III's celebration, which took place in 1809, had been the first proper Royal Jubilee that Britain had ever known. It had combined biblical references with a vogue for decadence to produce a party designed to include everyone in the country. As Queen Victoria prepared for her own anniversary, it also became a template which went on to inform the royal celebrations of the twentieth and twenty-first centuries.

The scarcity of Royal Jubilees until the nineteenth century had a lot to do with the ancient origin of the idea. Jubilees traditionally marked fifty years and medieval mortality meant few monarchs made that milestone. They were also largely religious festivals and the idea of aligning this spiritual celebration with temporal rulers remained unexplored.

Jubilees were first mentioned in the Old Testament in the Book of Leviticus. There, orders to let land lie fallow every seventh year were followed by a command that after seven cycles of seven years, the 'fiftieth year shall be a jubilee year to you'. It was to be a time of divine benevolence and feasting. The land was to be left to itself and anything it provided was to be enjoyed by all. This Jubilee year also saw all property returned to its rightful owners, slaves set free and sins forgiven. After the celebrations, the cycle of seven sets of seven years began again. The start of the Jubilee was sounded on a 'yobhel' or ram's horn. As the world 'jubilee' entered common parlance, its origins were traced back to that ram's horn.

The importance of fifty was carried forward by early Christians. Pentecost was seen as the Church's birthday from earliest times as the New Testament described the Holy Spirit descending on the Apostles as they marked the Jewish festival which fell fifty days after Passover. By the early thirteenth century, the number fifty was firmly associated with forgiveness and remission and held a certain sanctity. In England, the relics of St Thomas à Becket were moved to a new tomb within Canterbury Cathedral on the fiftieth anniversary of his murder, while scattered records show a handful of the longest lived monks marking a 'Jubilee' of their vocation after half a century. The monastic language, Latin, also provided a verb, *iubilare* meaning 'to shout with joy'.

But the concept of a Jubilee remained confined to the Church. While royal courts marked high days and holidays with pageantry, there was little concept of widespread celebrations linked to regal anniversaries. In England, the number of years that the current monarch had ruled often informed the recording of dates and it wasn't until the middle of the thirteenth century that any king reigned long enough for that number to reach fifty.

The first English king to mark a half century of rule was Henry III. He had been a boy king, taking the throne in 1216 at the age of nine. For the first decade of his reign he was at the whim of regency councils so, in effect, his personal rule hadn't really started until 1227. However, by the time the fiftieth anniversary of his accession came around, he was in no place to celebrate anyway. Henry had been taken captive in 1265 during the Second Barons' War and had only just been freed by his son and heir, Edward, as the fiftieth year of his reign got under way. The king was more concerned with consolidating his power than marking milestones. Besides, Henry was a pious man, devoted to the Church and the cult of St. Edward the Confessor in particular, and Jubilees belonged to the sphere of religion. The word was known to Bible scholars and religious people but the idea of it as a universal celebration was far from ingrained.

However, it wasn't unknown. Three decades after Henry III's fiftieth anniversary, Cardinal Giacomo Gaetani Stefaneschi, a close adviser of Pope Boniface VIII, would write of a swell of pilgrims coming to Rome as the thirteenth century drew to a close, some of them speaking of past 'jubilees'. Stefaneschi reported that one man, claiming to be 108 years old, had approached Boniface himself to share memories of his own visit to Rome one hundred years earlier when his sins, along with those of many others, were forgiven in a special celebration.

Other contemporary chronicles noted a steady increase in pilgrims to Rome in 1299, drawn there by a popular belief that the fourteenth century would be a time of exceptional hope and the best place to be as it began was the Eternal City. Pope Boniface, who had seen his power and wealth eroded in the previous few years by the ever growing ambitions of King Philip IV of France, had soon pulled together a plan to make the most of this swell in numbers. On 22 February 1300, the feast of the Chair of St. Peter, he issued a papal bull entitled *Antiquorum habet fida relatio* which proclaimed a special year for the Church. Anyone who made the trip to Rome, repented of their sins and then visited the Basilicas of St. Peter and St. Paul Without the Walls for fifteen days would be granted forgiveness.

Although the bull of Boniface VIII drew on the celebrations described in Leviticus, at no point did he call this year a 'jubilee'. However, others did. Stefaneschi wrote an account of the year soon after it had ended, *Liber de centesimo sive Jubileo*. Dante was one of the hundreds of thousands drawn to Rome and later included the *Giubileo* in his Inferno.

Both men reported the large numbers of pilgrims who took Boniface up on his promise of remission from sin in return for a pilgrimage to Rome. Stefaneschi noted one day where 30,000 pilgrims made their penance. The Old Testament sense of remission at a time of Jubilee touched hundreds of thousands of souls who went to Rome, while the feasting described by Leviticus was helped by the generosity of the local population and the decision of the city authorities to keep prices for pilgrims reasonable.

It led to a huge success. Boniface's spiritual influence was restored while the papal coffers also benefitted from the steady flow of contributions, but what made this a true Jubilee was the popular participation. Just as Leviticus had described a celebration that embraced all in society, so this first Jubilee year was open to all who were prepared to make the journey to Rome for their faith. The Papacy had ordered and organised it but it had done so against a background of popular demand and enthusiastic participation.

Pope Boniface decided that this special year should be repeated once a century. However, by the 1340s there was pressure for a return to the Old Testament notion of a Jubilee every fifty years. Leading philosophers including Petrarch complained to Pope Clement VI that life expectancy meant very few would get the chance to see a Jubilee and so claim the forgiveness that it might bring. Clement, then at Avignon as papal power fragmented, decreed 1350 to be a Jubilee year. Despite pressure for him to return to Rome for the event, he sent a cardinal to mark it for him in the mean streets of a city still divided by rival claims for papal power. The length between celebrations was altered several times in the following century until, in 1470, Pope Paul II settled on a period of twenty-five years for a Jubilee, a pattern followed in the main by the Catholic Church ever since.

However, the concept of the Jubilee remained indelibly linked to the Church despite some temporal rulers seeing its potential. Edward

III marked his fiftieth birthday in 1362 by issuing a general pardon in a clear reference to the Biblical focus of remission at a Jubilee. That link to the Biblical Jubilee, which had been used so spectacularly by the Papacy through the fourteenth century, was the first association of English royalty with a celebration they would end up making their own. It also reflected a growing acceptance of the term 'jubilee' as a mark of fifty years – a notable number of English knights had travelled to Rome for the second papal celebration of 1350, meaning the word and the concept were discussed at court.

In 1377 Edward and his advisers went one step further and used the term 'jubilee' in a sermon to mark the fiftieth anniversary of his accession on 25 January. The previous year, the Good Parliament had seen the Commons draw up a long list of concerns over the way the country was being governed. By the time of Edward's anniversary, opposition to royal rule was fragmenting once more, but as Bishop Houghton of St. David's preached the sermon to a new parliament about to meet, he made reference to the completion of the King's Jubilee, and as part of that, a new pardon would be issued if the Commons showed themselves worthy of it. They agreed and requested forgiveness. Other events, including a joust to mark the ailing King's anniversary, were also staged. The Royal Jubilee, although in a very muted form, had been born.

However, no other English sovereign would reach a half century of rule for another four hundred and fifty years. Elizabeth I came close, with a reign that extended for forty-five years, and her well-honed knack for self promotion saw her hold special celebrations linked to her royal majesty, but even her Armada tours, which incorporated visits to a string of castles in England for days of feasting and pageantry to mark the defeat of the Spanish navy, had limited popular involvement and never encompassed celebrations across her whole realm at the same time.

By the early seventeenth century, Jubilees were very definitely Catholic events. Elizabeth left her throne to King James of Scotland who had ruled that country since soon after his first birthday in 1567. The fiftieth year of his Scottish reign saw him return home for the first time since taking the English throne in 1603 but his focus then was on religious reform there rather than religious symbolism in the form of a Jubilee. His own belief in the divine right of kings would lead his son and successor, Charles I, towards Civil War and execution. The monarchy in England revived but threats to the very notion of royal rule remained and as these found a new voice, the creation of the first full scale British Jubilee began to take shape in the minds of royalists.

As the nineteenth century began, a woman called Rachel Charlotte Biggs became concerned about the level of opposition to the monarchy. King George III had put aside the early controversies of his reign and produced a patriarchal image for himself as he aged, but he had also produced a string of scandalous sons who seemed incapable of avoiding self destruction. In March 1809 his second child, Frederick, Duke of York quit as commander-in-chief of the Army after becoming embroiled in a cash for honours scandal. Mrs Biggs could take no more and decided something had to be done.

She later wrote that the anger surrounding the Duke of York's latest fall from grace had reminded her of the stirrings of radicalism that had led to the French Revolution of 1789 and the subsequent Terror, an event she had witnessed first hand. The bloody end of the French monarchy cast a shadow for all those loyal to other European crowns, as did the rise of radical thinkers and the newspapers and press that supported them. Mrs Biggs had a solution.

Thomas Brudenell-Bruce, Earl of Ailesbury, Treasurer to the King's wife, Queen Charlotte, happened to be one of her friends. She wrote to him suggesting George III set off on a tour of his kingdom to show his people, up close, just how much he cared for them. The Earl politely told her that the king was too ill to undertake such an endeavour. Undaunted, the determined Mrs Biggs moved on to Plan B. The King would have to have a Jubilee.

Since medieval times, there had been widespread debate about whether a Jubilee should be held when fifty whole years had been completed or at the start of the fiftieth year itself. Mrs Biggs was typically decisive. King George III would begin the fiftieth year of his reign on 25 October 1809 and he would do it in style. Her proposal for celebratory events replicated by communities across the kingdom was the most ambitious royal commemoration ever. There would be feasting and special services, balls and fireworks. The monarch would be placed at the centre of a moment of national unity and so cement the Crown at the heart of Britain.

Spurred on by her fervent loyalty to the Throne, Mrs Biggs settled down at her desk to write around 1,000 anonymous letters. They were addressed to the great and the good of cities, towns and villages around the country and they called on them to arrange local participation in a Jubilee celebration for the King that autumn. Mrs Biggs would later explain that she had attempted to make all the letters different to avoid suspicion that they came from the same source. But they followed the same, basic template. After extolling the almost unique achievement of George III in attaining five decades on the throne, Mrs Biggs rallied her readers to make sure this historic moment was marked appropriately.

> [I]t is, therefore, proposed as a mark of personal attachment to His Majesty, and totally unconnected with parties or politics, to celebrate the day by a national jubilee, or festival, throughout the United Kingdom. Such a fete must necessarily be subservient to local circumstances but where these do not interfere, review and public breakfasts in the morning, and balls and illuminations in the evening are recommended.

This homespun start to the great celebration wasn't quite as rudimentary as it seemed. Mrs Biggs was certainly filled with passion and determination but she also had good contacts. As well as the Earl of Ailesbury, she counted a certain John Reeves among her friends. He was the superintendent of the part of the Home Office which was in charge of managing the arrival of all 'aliens' into Britain. Mrs Biggs took several trips from her home near Chepstow to Bath where she sent off bulk batches of letters to Reeves who then put them in the post with London marks on them.

There was no time to rest for Charlotte Biggs. As well as starting to design her own perfect Jubilee, she also began a press campaign. Yet more letters were sent to provincial papers, outlining the exciting Jubilee plans already in place in rival cities and towns in the hope that these often made-up extravaganzas would spur vain aldermen into creating their own Jubilee plans to keep up with their rivals. Mrs Biggs used a string of different names for these early press releases and her plans began to bear fruit. The papers carried her letters while the provincial press also took the opportunity to use Jubilee ideas to pad out its papers in the slower weeks.

However, the idea wasn't universally popular. The enthusiastic Mrs Biggs was preaching to a country in the middle of the Napoleonic Wars. By the summer of 1809, the papers were also carrying details of the major losses sustained by British troops at Talavera de la Reina in Spain. Soon afterwards came the first reports of a terrible disease ripping through the large British troop presence at Walcheren in the Netherlands. The illness would eventually claim 4,000 lives while the military campaign that had taken them there faltered. Many were mourning, while the cost of living for homes across Britain was rising. The call for 'balls and illuminations' wasn't met with widespread joy.

The earliest critics of plans for the Jubilee seized on the proposals for 'illuminations'. By the early nineteenth century, the habit of lighting up homes and businesses for major events or to support a cause was a popular one, but it was also controversial. It cost money and, in some instances, those who decided not to participate were labelled agitators and found their darkened windows smashed.

As town and village leaders across the country began to call for people to light up their homes to mark the Jubilee, letters appeared in radical newspapers asking who would pay for the indulgence. One, sent to *The Independent Whig*, questioned why the poor should have to 'illuminate their miserable mansion' for a Royal Jubilee. The fact that the price of candles began to rise as the celebration plans took hold only added to criticisms. In early spring of 1809, tallow merchants began to build up reserves in anticipation of a run on candles around the time of the King's anniversary as people, regardless of devotion to the Crown, would be expected to light their windows for George III. Prices started to rise while some big organisations, including the Bank of England, quietly increased their candle reserves ahead of the Jubilee. Soon, that was seen by some as a sign of a more sinister operation.

The run on candles and the striking similarity of some of the letters sent to the press about Jubilee celebrations led to speculation that some kind of conspiracy was afoot. The same radical newspapers now questioned whether the whole Jubilee enterprise was a plan to try and divert the general population from the difficulties of war and poverty. Others argued that it was all a plot by businesses to make yet more money from those described by one radical journalist as 'the infatuated people'.

Through all the criticism, Mrs Biggs remained undetected and undeterred and her plans for a party to mark the royal reign continued to grow. On 4 June 1809, celebrations for the King's birthday in Bombay saw ambassadors from across the Indian Empire converge on the city for a huge fete, billed as a Jubilee. Councillors and aldermen began to discuss the type of feast they would hold and the kind of tributes they would make to George III at this auspicious moment.

It was then that the critics became creative. As radical journalists filled their papers with attacks on plans for so much frippery, they started to offer alternative suggestions for anyone who wanted to spend money to mark the Jubilee. The ideas soon caught hold. A letter to *The*

*Times* proposed that those authorities with money to spend on feasts and parties could, instead, devote the cash to a better cause and use it to pay off sums owed by those languishing in debtors' prisons. Another letter to the same paper suggested individuals could use the money they might spend on candles to donate to a campaign to build almshouses.

The ideas soon took hold with proponents directly referencing the Biblical Jubilees which had seen debts forgiven and sinners pardoned. Just as Mrs Biggs' appeal for a universal celebration was noted and debated across the country, so too were these calls for charity to be placed at the heart of the Jubilee. The letters pages of newspapers were soon filled with ideas of who should be helped to mark the Jubilee. The references to Biblical times soon led to increased calls for pardons for prisoners. Just days before the Jubilee, a general pardon for military deserters was issued while the new Prime Minister, Spencer Perceval, persuaded King George III to hand over money from his privy purse for the relief of debtors.

Almost eighty years later, as he tried to explain the past Jubilee to a Victorian population about to mark their own celebration, Thomas Preston of the Royal Historical Society noted that the King's donation was matched by others. George III, said Preston, gave £4,000 with the Corporation of London adding another £2,000 and the City Merchants and Bankers throwing in £1,000. Preston's 'Jubilee Jottings' also noted that while this was the only national subscription in 1809, similar charitable events took place across the nation, at local and community levels.

While the build up to the Jubilee was marked by political controversy and some questioning of the celebration's validity, the day itself ended up an impressive success. It was aided, in part, by the weather which, as Preston describes, 'broke brightly'. It was unseasonably sunny and mild throughout the day which was declared a holiday. With dry weather and the promise of celebration, many headed out to join their local Jubilee.

Not that they had much choice. The residents of Axminster were woken early on Jubilee morning by the church choir who, along with a band, had crammed themselves into the top of the church tower to start the day with a rendition of Handel's Coronation Anthem. They made their way down and paraded through the streets singing 'God Save the King, May the King Live Forever' before the local Yeoman Cavalry joined in with a *feu de joie*. In Newport, on the Isle of Wight, Jubilee Day had barely begun when musicians took to the streets to start singing in the celebrations while the civic leaders of Lichfield waited only for all twelve chimes of midnight to be struck before they began a parade, complete with band, to regale their fellow citizens with 'God Save the King'.

This noisy start was repeated across the country. In Plymouth and Stafford, choirs took to the church towers to sing in the Jubilee and other parishes found themselves woken by musicians performing 'God Save the King'. Bells began to peal, often keeping up their melodies for the whole day. In Bakewell, Derbyshire, the early morning chimes were followed by a gun salute of ten rounds while in St. Ives, Huntingdonshire, the bells were followed by 'firing cannon'. In Reading, it was gunfire that heralded the Jubilee Day with the Royal Berkshire Militia firing three volleys in the market place just as day broke. The residents of Portsmouth were also treated to 'the discharge of fifty guns' to start their Jubilee celebrations.

The schedule for celebrations looked rather like the suggestions enclosed in the anonymous letters sent by Mrs Biggs all those months earlier. Although a Wednesday, many put on their Sunday best to head to a service to give thanks for the King's long life and reign. The Archbishop of Canterbury wrote a special prayer and this spiritual statement was given temporal backing when the Privy Counsel formally issued it ahead of the Jubilee. It touched on the difficulties George III had overcome since ascending the throne in 1760 as well as asking for continued support for his rule.

> O God, in whose hands are the issues of life and death and to whom alone it belongeth to distribute mercies as

> well as in lengthening as in shortening the days of men, we yield thee praise and thanksgiving for the protection thou hast vouchsafed to our Gracious Sovereign, during a long and arduous reign.

The Chief Rabbi also wrote a Jubilee prayer which was said at the Great Synagogue, while services of all denominations across the country ended with 'God Save the King'. George III's early reign had seen the Gordon riots in which buildings with Catholic links had been attacked, but on the morning of his Jubilee, a specially written prayer was offered in Catholic churches for the King. In London, Catholic leader Joseph Hodgson told his fellow clerics that '*in these happy isles, we have enjoyed an enviable security in our own houses, while in other countries, everything sacred and profane, altars and thrones, have been thrown into the common mass of ruin.*'

His words echoed the sentiments of many who had been persuaded to join in Jubilee celebrations despite initial misgivings. Through the complaints over cost and the debate over the propriety of partying at a time of wars and tribulations, there had been voices arguing that while the long reign of George III had included difficult times, in comparison to other European nations, his realm was faring well.

As people came out of their homes to celebrate his Jubilee, Church service was followed by civic tributes with gatherings at guildhalls and town halls across Britain for the reading of a congratulatory address. All spoke directly to the King and heaped praise on him for the achievements of his reign.

In Shrewsbury, the Mayor, Aldermen and Burgesses all came together to tell the king that '*by the protection of divine provenance, Your Majesty has been preserved to us from the machinations of secret, and from the Attacks of open Enemies, through a Reign arduous, eventful and of Duration nearly unexampled in our Annals*', while in Dorchester, the salutation said that all were '*truly thankful for the Happiness and Tranquillity which we have enjoyed under Your Majesty's mild and paternal Government; and gratefully acknowledge that it is to Your Majesty's exemplary virtues, under Favour of Divine Providence, that we owe our Preservation from the dreadful Calamities which have overwhelmed the rest of Europe.'*

The leading lights of Hertford told King George III that *'we are truly sensible of the illustrious example which Your Majesty, during a long and arduous reign, has displayed to all Ranks of your people, and we trust that Divine Providence will continue to preserve Your Majesty on a Throne which you have adorned with your religious, moral and social Virtues'*, while in York, the advances of industry were laid at George's door, as the elders told him *'our arts, manufactures and commerce have, under Your Majesty's Auspices, arrived at a Degree of Perfection, which has tended to increase and spread the Fame and Importance of this Nation.'*

Every salutation was inscribed on parchment and sent to the King via the Home Secretary. George III will have found a replication of wishes on the addresses with many praising his fatherly presence and virtues before reminding him, in great number, that his reign had been arduous as well as long.

In the major cities of George III's British realm, the celebrations took on an even more formal aspect. In Edinburgh, a huge procession made its way through the city streets led by the Society of High Constables, followed by the Lord Provost, the Grand Lodge of Freemasons of Scotland and members of the Navy. The ships in dock were decked with flags while many vessels were home to temporary scaffolding which was packed with people trying to get the best possible view of the celebrations. The first stone of a new bastion was laid and newspaper reports estimated the crowd in the city to be around 20,000 for these Jubilee celebrations.

The Chancellor of the University of Oxford led his fellows as he offered '*our most humble and sincere congratulations on an Event in its Nature so extraordinary as to have been but seldom recorded in the History of Other Nations and to have occurred to a very few only in the long series of Your Majesty's Predecessors'.*

That reference to the rarity of Jubilees was a reminder of the unique nature of this royal celebration. But while there was little precedent for it, people across Britain were entering into the spirit of the party with some gusto. London, which had been the centre of many of the most fervent objections to the Jubilee, also saw many of the biggest celebrations. The Common Council of the City of London had heard vigorous arguments about the appropriateness of several planned jubilations, including protests at the idea of a church service, a loyal address and, in particular, a huge banquet. However, as Jubilee Day dawned, the crowds around Leadenhall were so big that several newspapers described the streets as 'impassable'.

They were treated to a magnificent parade, headed by the Lord Mayor, Charles Flower, who made his way from the Mansion House to Guildhall in the City State Coach, drawn by six grey horses decked with ribbons. He was met there by the Corporation and a new procession began to St. Paul's Cathedral where the dignitaries were met by the West London Militia before a service lasting several hours got under way.

Noticeably absent from the celebrations in the capital was the star of the Jubilee show. King George III spent this historic day at Windsor, where he now resided with only rare forays into public life. Jubilee Day would be no different. George's only actual participation in this nationwide party was to inspect a guard of soldiers and to take a carriage ride down the Long Walk. Along with his consort, Queen Charlotte, and several of their children, he also attended a private service at St. George's Chapel but was heard to speak ruefully to one of his sons about his failing eyesight which stopped him enjoying the full spectacle put on in his honour.

The Royal Family, with Charlotte at their head, made sure to enjoy the large scale celebrations in Windsor itself, passing beneath a ceremonial arch erected at the Guildhall. They also went to an ox roast set up at Bachelor's Wood at Windsor, enjoying the event from a specially built stand. An enormous spit and fire had been set up to cook the ox along with two large sheep which had also been donated for the celebrations. Much to the delight of loyalists everywhere, Queen Charlotte chose to walk through these celebrations on the arm of her second son, Frederick, giving the disgraced Duke of York a rare royal honour on this most important of days. Mrs Biggs, who had been inspired to start her Jubilee project because of Frederick, would have been amongst the most impressed.

Queen Charlotte was given first taste of the ox and declared herself very happy with it. The royal party then headed back to the castle while the meat was distributed amongst the crowd. *The Times* reported that almost as soon as the Queen had left, organisers began to throw the food to those clamouring to take part in the celebrations with some participants ending up with gravy on their heads.

The feasts that were laid on for this first British Royal Jubilee were among the most anticipated of all the celebrations. Often, they were provided by local nobility. The opposition to the idea of needless extravagance at the Jubilee had led to feeding the poor being a major priority. In Evesham, the Earl of Coventry donated an ox to be roasted and distributed among the poor with widows promised four pounds of beef on Jubilee Day. Sir J.C Hippesley, Sudbury's MP, provided £100 for a feast for poorer residents with subscribers bringing in another £200 for the party. In Devizes, those considered needy enough were treated to beef, potatoes and beer which was brought to their homes.

The residents of Stroud subscribed to an appeal to provide a feast for the poor to mark Jubilee Day and raised enough money to buy over 5,000 pounds of meat which was shared among 5,000 paupers. In Towcester, the Town Crier took to the streets the day before the Jubilee to announce a meal for the poor of the town which was attended by over 1,000 people. The feast's organiser, Gilbert Flesher, supervised a thorough clean-up afterwards, piling up all the leftovers at his own house and distributing them the day after the Jubilee to maximise the charitable reach of this royal anniversary.

Everyone was to partake of the Jubilee feast. In Derby, prisoners were given roast beef and plum pudding, paid for by the High Sheriff. The poorest children in Falmouth were treated to a special meal. Meanwhile, the town hosted parties which went on into the evening. A ninety foot long table was constructed in Petersham to allow as many residents as possible to dine together in honour of King George III. This first Jubilee also featured bunting-strewn tables as the roast beef at the heart of the feast held in Norwich was carried to the table with a Union flag above it with the dish placed beneath a portrait of Lord Nelson.

Among those celebrating the Jubilee were thousands of debtors, freed from prisons after public fundraising was used to bring in the money to pay off their debts. Those most opposed to the Jubilee as an extravagance had focused much of their efforts on redirecting money put aside for the celebrations towards paying off debts. George III himself gave £4,000 to the national fund while thousands more was raised at local levels. In Sheffield, all the prisoners of the Courts of Requests were pardoned and sent home on the night of 24 October 1809 so they could make full use of the Jubilee Day. In Newcastle, the anniversary began with six debtors being released from jail. In Lancaster, the funds raised allowed two prisoners to have their debts repaid while the sole debtor in Swansea Jail was also given freedom to mark the start of the fiftieth year of George III's reign.

The King had issued a general amnesty for all military deserters ahead of his Jubilee. The pardon for those who had run away from the Navy gave them full freedom. Army deserters were pardoned and freed from the threat of punishment, but they did have to sign up again. Meanwhile, a general amnesty for all military prisoners was also declared.

The benevolence extended to some prisoners of war. Tens of thousands were either in jail or on parole and as part of his Jubilee,

George III pardoned all of them – except the French. In Reading, around 200 Danish prisoners were marched to the Market Place where they were told they were free again. In Lichfield, the newly released prisoners were treated to a special meal while in Portsmouth they were given cash and a commemorative card. Meanwhile, fundraisers gathered cash for British prisoners being held in jails overseas.

King George III was well enough to dictate some of the terms of the pardons he issued, insisting with all his royal majesty that the Biblical theme of remission shouldn't extend to anyone who had shown themselves to be in any way delinquent and despite his physical absence from the main celebrations, as evening fell on his Jubilee day, his presence was felt everywhere. The illuminations that Mrs Biggs had urged the country to put on in his honour began to light the autumn twilight and among the displays were thousands of transparencies, many of them featuring a likeness of the king.

The illuminations, so controversial beforehand, became a spectacular end to the day. The Bank of England was adorned with lanterns that took a team of lighters over five hours to prepare. The sparkling lights picked out wreaths wrapped around its famous columns while in the centre was a star and crown and the words 'God Save the King'. Across London, famous buildings were lit up with Lloyds erecting a representation of a ship called the Jubilee on its façade. The Ordnance Office displayed a transparency bearing the guardian angel of Britain supporting King George and Queen Charlotte, while the front of Vauxhall Gardens was covered in lamps in the form of a temple of loyalty. East India Dock House bore illuminations spelling out G.R. while West India House was adorned with an illumination of 'Long Live the King' and The Admiralty had each of its pillars adorned with spiralling, multi coloured lamps.

At Frogmore, Queen Charlotte's beloved house in the grounds of Windsor Castle, more illuminations decorated a temporary bridge built over the lake as part of a tableau that took centre stage in an evening of entertainment. Fireworks were set off, reflecting in the water, their effect magnified by the continuing still, clear weather. Boats with actors representing tritons sailed across the water while two chariots appeared from the lake. In the centre of the lake was an island with a temple, topped by a bust of George III.

It summed up the role of the King in his Jubilee. George had been a silent partner in this great celebration even though it only existed because of him. The bust of him at Frogmore, like the images used of him in the thousands of transparencies that decorated towns and cities, showed him in his prime, the mature monarch who had become patriarch, the sins of his early reign long forgiven. The King who was feted at this Jubilee was the perfect personification of his monarchy, an object of easy admiration whose long life and service was being celebrated despite the politicians and princes who had let him down in later years.

In an 'Account of the Celebration of the Jubilee' by 'the Wife of a Naval Officer', published soon after the event, it was claimed that the Jubilee 'once expressed, moved with a rapidity almost unexampled, and what was the act of millions was the spontaneous effusion of love in each individual'. The celebrations had run into opposition but, in the end, had achieved their original aim and created a nationwide event that had rejoiced in royalty and shown it in its best light.

The Jubilee of George III had been created, in several different ways, by the people who celebrated it. While opponents of a nationwide party criticised the excess of the ideas pushed by Mrs Biggs, they didn't question stopping them in their tracks. Instead, they asked for changes that reflected their ideas of what a Jubilee should be. Inherent in many of their demands was the question of what Britain should look like to the rest of the world. Although unspoken, the notion of a Jubilee as a moment of unity had been established.

The timing of his Jubilee proved fortuitous. Whether Mrs Biggs' sense of urgency had been informed by the King's health as much as her concerns that revolution was about to engulf his realms isn't clear. Just as no one really knows why she was able to command the attention of some of the most important people in the land given her relatively obscure background, there is no concrete evidence that she knew enough about the King's declining health to make the start of his fiftieth year the object of her Jubilee plans. But it was a wise decision. By the time the fiftieth anniversary of George's reign arrived, he was seriously ill again. The loss of his beloved daughter, Princess Amelia, soon afterwards caused further decline. His mental health was soon so poor that another Regency was established. He would never rule in his own right again.

His eldest son, now Prince Regent, continued to spend money at an alarming rate and to drag his personal life through the public sphere, to almost universal ridicule. Meanwhile, the Crown was in the midst of a succession crisis. The Prince Regent's only heir, Princess Charlotte of Wales, had been a popular success at the Jubilee celebrations, feted at her appearances and positioned as the hope of the monarchy. But in 1817 she had died giving birth to a stillborn son. George III's long reign, marked by Britain's first real royal Jubilee, was drawing to a close with no second generation to inherit his throne.

The beginning of the sixtieth year of George III's reign came on 2 October 1819. By then, the King had long been confined to Windsor Castle. The dissolute sons who had alarmed Mrs Biggs into a push for royal PR that had culminated in the Jubilee had dashed around Europe looking for suitable brides and, by the time of the sixtieth anniversary, had begun to produce a new raft of grandchildren who might, one day, succeed to the throne. As George III whiled away the fifty-ninth anniversary of his accession at Windsor, one of them had just turned five months old.

Princess Alexandrina Victoria of Kent was fifth in line to her grandfather's throne at the time and it is likely that George, in his illness, had no awareness she had even been born. He died on 29 January 1820. Almost seventy years later, that same princess would turn the Royal Jubilee into a global event marking not just her personal rule but the success of a global dominion that had led to her being named Empress.

## Chapter Two

# Queen Victoria's Golden Jubilee

As 1887 got under way, Queen Victoria unwrapped a New Year present from her heir. Sitting in her rooms at Osborne, where she had spent the festive season, she pulled ribbons away from the gift and was rather amused at what she found. The Prince of Wales had sent her a Jubilee inkstand. It was shaped as a crown and when the queen opened it, she found a model of her own head. She declared it 'pretty and useful'. By the end of the year, the same would be said of the royal event that dominated it, her Golden Jubilee.

In large part, that would be down to Victoria. The Queen would have some choice words about the celebrations as plans unfolded to mark her half century of rule, but as soon as she gave her blessing to the idea of a Jubilee, she was determined to do it her way and that blessing had come a long time before the celebrations. As early as February 1886 Victoria was talking about her Golden festivities as a done deal, noting in her journals that her sadness over parting with her second son, Alfred, as he headed overseas with the military was mitigated by the knowledge that he would return for her Jubilee the following year.

In fact, the date when she would celebrate her half century had been one of the first moments when she had made her personality felt. The only previous proper Jubilee in Britain had adhered to Biblical tradition and been held at the start of the fiftieth year of royal rule. Victoria dismissed that out of hand. Her celebration would mark a complete fifty years and in the fractious political set up of the time, she found support from the Liberals.

One of their leading figures, Earl Granville, seemed to take on an aspect of Charlotte Biggs who had generated the very concept of Royal Jubilee at the start of the nineteenth century and helped propel it into being with her endless energy. Mrs Biggs had wanted the celebrations to seem like a spontaneous outbreak of rejoicing in a beloved monarch. Earl Granville hinted at similar motives. In March 1886, he wrote 'the idea should come from the outside…if it is taken up, then the government could do what they can to help it'.

However, Lord Granville was also motivated by money. From the earliest days of planning the official celebrations there were intense debates about who would pay for the showpiece events. The first British Royal Jubilee had seen local agencies and well resourced organisations shell out for the large scale festivities in London, corporation sponsorship ensuring that Jubilee became reality.

That was made easier by King George III being confined to his castle at Windsor. The main celebrations involving him were a short religious service within the castle walls and a brief inspection of a guard of honour within the estate's grounds. There was no pressure on the machinery of state to fund set piece celebrations with the Monarch at their heart. The Jubilee had been established as a way of local areas celebrating the figurehead who brought them together as a nation. Almost a century on, things looked rather different.

Victoria, although never shy about complaining of the physical ailments that age brought, was actually in rather good health, even if her mobility slowed as the years wore on. There was no reason not to make her the star of the show. This would be Britain's first Royal Jubilee featuring the royals themselves.

Her well pronounced ego, often hidden behind her widow's weeds, was another reason to expect the Queen to take central stage in the proceedings. Victoria always referred to the celebrations as 'my Jubilee'. Her household took the hint. On the forty-ninth anniversary of her reign, and the start of her fiftieth year, she was at Balmoral where she was presented with a large floral arrangement by 'all my ladies and gentlemen' while the wise and diplomatic minister, Mr Campbell, ensured his sermon that day was all about the Queen.

Victoria's journal entry for 20 June 1886, the day she might have marked her Jubilee, noted that she was 'very thankful and encouraged by these marks of affection and appreciation of my efforts'. Encouraged was an interesting interpretation of the events for this anniversary of her accession for Victoria was well aware that the success of her Jubilee was, at this stage, by no means guaranteed. It had been almost eighty years since her grandfather's celebrations and much had changed. The decision of the Royal Historical Society to publish a booklet explaining how a popular celebration of a Jubilee unfolded only underlined that the Queen, along with her advisers, was stepping into something of an unknown.

The only previous Jubilee was no real guide. Victoria's grandfather, George III, had been all but absent from his Golden celebrations in 1809. His image had appeared around the country on plaques and transparencies and medals but the King himself had been confined to his oldest castle while his queen and an assortment of their children, several of them in disgrace, headed out to greet the crowds.

The first British Jubilee had happened around a father-like fairy tale, placed at its centre by enthusiastic supporters who wanted to bolster the Crown as a whole. As a new matriarch of the Monarchy approached her own anniversary, the question of how to actually incorporate the Jubilee Queen into the Jubilee was hotly debated, as was how this royal show might actually be received by the public. That partly explained the government's increasing reluctance to fund the extravaganza. The set piece celebrations would cost a lot of money and, if they flopped, ministers were open to charges of wasting precious public funds. Besides, the earliest plans for the central events included most of the crowned heads of Europe and many of their families. They were nearly all related to Victoria, which gave politicians a good reason to ask the Jubilee monarch to fund her Jubilee herself.

The shape of the celebration was another major concern for Victoria from the very earliest days of planning. In the autumn of 1886, her private secretary wrote to the Prime Minister, Lord Salisbury, to inform him that the Queen would be taking part in a religious service to mark her anniversary. It would be held at Westminster Abbey and Victoria was ready to go into battle over how it would unfold.

There would be nods to her Coronation, but Victoria would only go so far. Suggestions she wear a crown and her Robe of State were instantly dismissed despite the protestations of some of her family. Victoria knew how to get her own way and she knew just how she wanted to look on the day her Empire celebrated her reign. Just as she had every day since the death of her beloved husband, Prince Albert, in 1861, Victoria would wear black with a few trims of lace and maybe some diamonds. London would be decked in finery but the Queen would look virtually the same as she had for every day of the second half of her rule.

If the Queen planned to be personally low key at this high point of her reign, there was no question of the day itself being anything other than splendid. So many royal guests meant that glittering receptions and banquets were all but compulsory. When her private secretary first explained to Lord Salisbury just how the Queen saw her Jubilee, he added that even the alterations needed at the Abbey might be so expensive, they could require a vote in parliament. The Prime Minister was ready. He quickly set up a committee to manage preparations with the Queen promptly informed that the government would pay for preparing the Abbey for her Jubilee but everything else would come from her own purse.

Lord Salisbury would experience the Queen's passion for perfecting her Jubilee on more than one occasion. In March 1887, she noted in her journals that the Prime Minister had visited her not long after recovering from illness when he had been treated to a regal monologue on 'Jubilee arrangements, some of which he did not seem to understand, 'till I explained them to him'.

However, her premier gave as good as he got. His determination produced an extreme reaction from the Queen in one letter sent by her during the build-up when she told him she would not be 'bullied' on the matter of the Jubilee. Her own way was clearly hard to come by at this stage as she went on to complain that the whole extravaganza was being devised 'only for the people and their convenience'. It was true that 'the people' had certainly come round to the idea of a national celebration. Just as Victoria's diaries throughout late 1886 and early 1887 make regular references to discussions about 'my Jubilee' so people across the country were also starting to make preparations for the party to come.

As Victoria was unwrapping her Jubilee inkstand on New Year's Day in 1887, readers of the *Kentish Independent* were enjoying a review of a local pantomime in the January first edition which noted the play's references to the upcoming Jubilee. Theatre goers in Alnwick were already able to enjoy performances at the new Victoria, named in honour of the impending Jubilee, while the *Framlingham Weekly News* mentioned a recent protest against plans by school teachers to ask for an extra two weeks holiday in the summer to mark the Queen's anniversary.

However, the prevalence of regal celebrations was already starting to jar. An editorial in the *Leamginton Spa Courier* noted that '*the world begins a New Year, and better than that, a Jubilee year though, upon my word, that Jubilee threatens to disturb the peace of millions... everything, from a cup of spa water to a pound of prize-packet tea has the Jubilee benediction...upon it.*'

*The Globe* summarised the prevalence of Jubilee preparations with a comic turn in its New Year's Day edition. *'Jubilee, like plum pudding, is very filling and everyone tries to stuff it down our throats. Everything that man can eat, drink, wear or use is being baptised, or rebaptised, Jubilee.'*

The word Jubilee had entered common parlance and as the event it marked entered public consciousness, the concept found a willing audience. Britain and the Empire were ready to celebrate, albeit with some cherry picking.

Unsurprisingly perhaps, given the focus on who would pay for the main celebrations in London, there was markedly less interest in the Biblical Jubilee concept of pardoning sin and writing off debt. While marmalade magnate, J.M. Keiller, donated over £10,000 to clear the debts on Dundee Library and Museum at the start of Jubilee year, nods to this ancient tradition remained rare and personal. That was despite newspaper campaigns such as one suggested by the *Norwich Mercury* at the start of 1887 which noted the move in 1809 to use the Jubilee as a way of giving to the poor and which urged a return to the original concept of the celebration with the 'striking off of all the bonds' endured by agricultural workers. A widely syndicated letter from a vicar in London's East End urged all those who intended to spend on the Queen's celebrations to put aside some of those contributions for the poor.

However, there would be no widespread campaigning to write off monies owed by debtors or calls for pardons for the least troubling of criminals in Britain. Charity remained confined to the great and good of local areas entertaining the poor to a decent dinner to mark the event. In greater part, this Jubilee would leave behind the notion of remission that had accompanied it ever since Pope Boniface VIII had introduced it into western secular culture as the fourteenth century began.

Instead, there was far more of a focus on large scale fundraising. Giving to charity was all well and good but it had to tie in with the late Victorian focus on nation and empire. The Prince of Wales began a campaign for an Imperial Institute as part of his mother's Golden Jubilee. In the years before her celebrations, a string of exhibitions centred on India and the Colonies had proved popular and so, after some political wrangling, the Prince set up a fundraising campaign to create an Institute that would be a museum, an exhibition space and a place where all matters of empire could be discussed. He wrote to mayors and local dignitaries around the empire asking them to join the fundraising efforts while a competition to design the institute was launched. In the end, over £400,000 would be raised.

However, it provoked some clashes as local fundraisers looked to channel money towards other causes. A row broke out at the Okehampton Board of Guardians when they were asked, not for the first time, to raise funds for the Institute. Rebuking the demand as 'outside their duties', there were some scathing remarks about the Queen being very far from a pauper. In the end, the town put on free teas and sports for children and left the glorification of empire to others.

Charity on a local level retained some of the focus of the first Jubilee as appeals were made to help those most in need at this time of celebration. In Soho, a certain Mr. Holt dipped his hand into his pockets to provide a generous meal for 500 poor widows, in honour of his widowed Queen. In York, a meal was laid on for the poor of the city with anyone in receipt of outdoor relief from York Union invited to a Jubilee celebration where they were given plenty to eat and drink in honour of the Queen. Meanwhile, one of the first Jubilee resolutions made in Sheerness in Kent was to provide a prodigious dinner for the poor to mark the anniversary.

But there were far more varied opportunities to splash the cash as this Jubilee took shape. Victoria's own excitement about the inkstand she received on New Year's Day was increased by the knowledge that this was the first of a mass batch that would wend its way around the country and the world as another Jubilee tradition made its debut: souvenir selling. The editorial in *The Globe* that appeared as she unwrapped her gift highlighted the mass marketing opportunities that this royal anniversary presented. Improvements in manufacture and transport made large scale production of trinkets easier and cheaper and Britain's businesses were ready to profit from their Queen's celebrations.

Mementoes such as cups, glasses and plates were in ready supply, usually bearing the Queen's image and her dates. The flip-top regalia of Victoria's inkstand was matched by perfume bottles with screw-top crowns. Terracotta ware, toys, trinket boxes and bracelets were found on sale everywhere. No business was immune from including a Jubilee touch to its offerings in the hope of cashing in. Mr Alfred Montgomery of John Street, London added a range of 'novelties for the Queen's jubilee' to his party business which already supplied entertainers, performing dogs and fireworks to all kinds of parties around the capital. Adverts for the rental of hot water boilers for Jubilee tea parties became commonplace as the big day approached.

As 1887 wore on, the word Jubilee was used to sell anything and everything. In Oxford Street, budding musicians could buy Jubilee and Victoria Jubilee Banjos from Brewsters, while a short stroll to Regent Street would take them to Cremer's where Jubilee balloons were readily available. Simpson's of Chelmsford offered Jubilee flowers and Jubilee mineral waters went on sale in Southend. In Belfast, adverts appeared for Jubilee furniture while Hodgson and Simpson of Wakefield promoted 'Queen's Jubilee Invincible Soap', which they promised was 'the finest and purest soap in the world'.

The first official Jubilee celebrations took place in India in February 1887, brought forward to avoid the heat that would prevail at the time of the actual anniversary of Victoria's reign in June. The Queen's third son, the Duke of Connaught, was present in Mumbai for the event which saw much of the city centre lit up by illuminations. A public holiday was declared while remnants of the Biblical essence of Jubilees would appear in June as Britain partied. On Jubilee Day itself in India, all debtors who owed 100 rupees or less were set free while around one third of those in jail were also set free for the anniversary. This garnered barely a mention in British newspapers where there was far more focus on Indian contributions to the Jubilee celebrations in London. Victoria was deeply interested in her empire and her Jubilee procession would include an escort of Indian cavalry who would ride in a prime position.

Invitations to the festivities had already been extended to princes from across India. Not all accepted but the Thakor of Limbdi, the Maharaja of Morvi, the Maharaja of Cooch Behar, the Maharao of

Kutch, the Thakor of Gondal and the Maharaja of Holkar of Indore joined her in London to mark her anniversary. They would be special guests in the Abbey and at Buckingham Palace throughout the celebrations and their elaborate gifts were also well documented in the press. An Arab stallion bedecked with gold and silver, presented by the Maharaja of Morvi, made quite an impression as did another of Victoria's imperial initiatives for her Jubilee.

Ahead of her celebrations, the queen asked for two Indian servants to be brought to her household where they would remain for a year. Mohammed Buksh arrived in England in June 1887 along with Abdul Karim. Their arrival raised eyebrows within the royal household and they only went higher as Karim quickly became a close confidante of the Jubilee Queen. By the time of her next Jubilee, in 1897, he would be such a non-negotiable part of her royal life that questions, not all of them polite, were being asked about his real role. However, in June 1887 he made a discreet entrance to Windsor Castle, barely noticed by the Queen who had the frantic business of her Jubilee to attend to.

Victoria had taken an unwavering interest in every aspect of her actual fiftieth anniversary as Queen. In March she sat with Mr. Parralt, the organist at Windsor, as he tried to practice '*dearest Albert's Te Deum which is to be performed at the Jubilee'*. The musician had to contend with a deteriorating organ as well as a mourning Queen as he attempted to get things ready for the celebrations.

Victoria had spent the weeks before the actual anniversary at Balmoral. On 24 May, she had celebrated her sixty-eighth birthday there, settling herself into the rooms used by Albert for the presentation of gifts, many of them sent to mark her Jubilee, too. However, the relentless nature of the celebrations was starting to make itself felt. Victoria noted '*I gave all my people Jubilee brooches and pins. No end to loyal telegrams.*'

A few days later, she received a letter from Downing Street describing in eye watering detail the service of thanksgiving recently held at St. Margaret's Church, Westminster and attended by the House of Commons. The vivid description of the inaugural procession, led by the Speaker in all his finery, was followed by an intricate explanation of the two and a half hour ceremony which followed. However, Victoria would have been less impressed with the news that the crowds gathered to watch the politicians included those ready to jeer as well as cheer.

Opposition to the Jubilee had arisen and not just in the jocular words of editorials which declared the decadence dull before it had even begun. The anniversary celebrations of Queen Victoria became the focus for protests against British rule in Ireland with a series of demonstrations taking place across the country as well as among Irish Americans in Boston. There were complaints, too, about the cost of the celebrations, highlighted in satirical poems which questioned the gushing prose that proclaimed the Jubilee Queen the foundation of all goodness. Satirical magazines questioned whether the party would turn into a washout as the big day approached.

Some of the complaints were mitigated by the financial benefits that the Jubilee brought with it. While Victoria would end up out of pocket, spending around £50,000 on her celebrations, others found themselves making money. A spate of hospital building to mark the Jubilee provided work for hundreds while even the most regal celebrations became job makers – the renovation of Frogmore House at Windsor to receive the Queen's guests at her Jubilee meant local employment opportunities for many.

As her royal relations prepared to make their way to Windsor and London, Victoria remained aloof in Scotland where she spent her last days of seclusion visiting nearby villages, handing out souvenirs of her celebrations and planting a tree to mark the occasion. She also agreed the design of a statue to be erected nearby to mark her anniversary, but as the June temperatures increased, she boarded the royal train to make her way to Windsor where she would begin her Royal Jubilee.

The actual anniversary of her accession, 20 June 1887, was a strange mix of private and public celebration. In the morning, Victoria took her closest relations for an outdoor breakfast close to the mausoleum where her beloved Albert now rested. She didn't have long to mourn times past. Under clear blue skies she headed to the train station, but despite the bustle of the day, there was time to admire the decorations decking Windsor for its Jubilee Queen. She arrived at Paddington where an open landau was waiting for her. But if Victoria had retained any reservations about the success of her Jubilee, they were soon forgotten. The short route to Buckingham Palace was packed with crowds, huge cheers greeting her on every stage of the journey.

The Queen made no secret of her loathing for the Palace which held little interest or affection for her, but it remained the seat of royal power and on the fiftieth anniversary of her accession, she found it packed with regal relations. Many, including her eldest grandson, Wilhelm of Prussia, were waiting to greet her after her train trip. They all joined her for lunch but there was no leisurely repast for Victoria. She was soon hurried off to give audiences before settling into the gardens of her London home to answer more telegrams. Then it was time to dress for dinner where she would host one of the largest gatherings of royalty in recent times.

Her journal for the night of 20 June 1887 famously records '*the King of Denmark took me in and Willy of Greece sat on my other side. The princes were all in uniform and the princesses were all beautifully dressed.*'

That belies the sheer breadth of European royalty that was gathered at Buckingham Palace that night. Victoria's Jubilee was attended by over fifty kings, queens, heirs, princes and princesses. Of course, she knew many of them for they called her mother or grandmother. Fifty years previously, she had inherited a fragile throne. Now, she had peopled Europe's royal houses and they had returned to her to mark her achievement.

And yet, in the midst of all this adulation, Victoria nursed her ever broken heart. Her first thought that morning had been *'the day has come and I am alone'* while she poignantly noted that the grand lunch on this first day of her celebrations was held in the Buckingham Palace dining room which she had not used since the year that Albert had died. However, if she hoped to sleep her sadness away, she was to be disappointed. The lonely Queen went to bed in a city packed with excited visitors who all wanted to be part of her Golden Jubilee, many of them singing loudly as midnight struck.

Hours later, they were packing stands and windows along the route of the Jubilee procession. For months before, spots along the parade were being advertised in newspapers and magazines and the best vantage points might have sold several times over, such was the interest. As this midsummer's day dawned, they were treated to an epic spectacle to mark the Jubilee. They were, in fact, treated to two processions with the assorted royal families of Europe making their way to the Abbey in one parade, while Victoria and her closest relations starred in the main show which saw ten state carriages ride ahead of the Queen and a troop of Life Guards close out the procession.

The Queen rode in a gilt landau drawn by six cream horses. Twelve Indian officers rode immediately in front, another reminder of her Empire. Her eldest daughter, now Crown Princess of Prussia, and her most senior daughter-in-law, the Princess of Wales, sat alongside her. Her three surviving sons, the Prince of Wales, the Duke of Edinburgh and the Duke of Connaught, went on horseback ahead of her with all five of her sons-in-law. An assortment of grandsons and grandsons-in-law also rode in the procession while daughters, granddaughters and in-laws packed out the carriages in the parade.

The Queen left Buckingham Palace under brilliant blue skies. She made her way along Constitution Hill, a familiar sight but one of unpleasant memories too for three assassination attempts had been made on Victoria on its long, straight course during her reign. The sun sparkled as she approached the gleaming white stones of what we now call Wellington Arch but which had only just welcomed a statue of Victoria's Prime Minister. Next to this monument to military might was a stand filled with Chelsea Pensioners in their bright red coats. She passed onwards to Piccadilly and the brand new Northumberland Avenue with its glamourous new hotels, including the Victoria, a magnet for American tourists.

The seemingly endless string of carriages wended its way on to the Embankment with Westminster Abbey now in sight. Every street was strung with flags and bunting and packed with spectators. The little Queen was almost lost among the pomp, dressed in black with some white lace in her bonnet. There were pearls and a few diamonds as well as the Order of the Garter and the Star of India, but Victoria had been true to her word and dressed as a widow rather than an empress. She was even outdressed by the Archbishop of Canterbury and the Dean of the Abbey who had both put on the velvet robes used by their predecessors at Victoria's coronation, forty-nine years earlier. And yet, as she hinted in her diaries, all this ceremony, all these royal guests, all this majesty was in existence for one reason only: to celebrate Victoria.

Except it was about much more, for while Victoria always referred to it as 'my Jubilee', she also spoke frequently of the 'great burden' and the 'great responsibility' of her role and would remind her subjects of her life of service when she issued her formal thanks for the celebrations. Victoria's 'I' was truly the royal 'I', encompassing millions in her personage.

All of that was hidden in a small waiting room put aside for her at the Abbey as her dozens of relatives and royal visitors arranged themselves into a truly spectacular parade of sovereign power. It began to wend its way through the ancient church, the usually cool air of the Abbey rendered powerfully warm by the thousands of people packed inside for the service. And then, came the Queen. The national anthem played, followed by Handel's Occasional Overture, as she walked slowly along the aisle. She approached her dozens of royal guests, the highest ranking seated within the altar rails, and took her place on the Coronation Chair for the service.

It was a poignant moment. Despite the thousands in the abbey and the multitude outside, Victoria would note, again, how very alone she felt.

The service, which included Albert's Te Deum, ended with her many royal relations paying homage to her, one by one, kissing her hand and making a bow or a curtsy. It held up the return procession considerably but Victoria dutifully drove back a different way to Buckingham Palace to allow as many well-wishers as possible to catch sight of her. They continued to celebrate outside while the Queen was absorbed back into the Palace for the presentation of more gifts, the bestowal of Jubilee pins on her dozens of guests and the reading of telegrams. There would be no rest in the evening as she changed into a gown embroidered in silver with roses, thistles and shamrocks and headed into another grand banquet.

The King of Denmark, her rival as parent of Europe's royal houses, raised a toast to her while her son, the Prince of Wales, proposed the health of the guests on behalf of his mother. Her European relations were then treated to a very Scottish celebration as pipers played their way around the table before the Queen went to the ballroom to receive her royal relations and the Indian princes as well as the Diplomatic Corps and foreign envoys.

When Victoria, by now exhausted, finally retired she was almost too tired to sleep. Instead, she tried to catch sight of the illuminations set up around her capital to mark her Jubilee but failed. However, she concluded the day had been a success, writing in her journal that she *'felt truly grateful that all had passed off so admirably'*.

However, a proper night's sleep was out of the question as the Jubilee party continued in London's streets. There had been celebrations across the country to mark the anniversary and many of them looked rather similar to the festivities for George III's Jubilee. Just as in 1809 beacons had been lit to mark the celebrations with bonfires springing into life around the country in homage to an ancient royal tradition of using fire to mark monarchical milestones.

One of the most popular ways of celebrating remained the ox roast, with local dignitaries donating the beast and other well-to-do residents providing beer, plum pudding and treats to go with it. In Tingewick in Buckinghamshire, the children of the village had formed a procession and marched through the lanes behind a brass band. A parade in Rushden in Hertfordshire included much of the local population, many carrying banners and flags and singing the national anthem. On arrival at their party in a nearby field, they sat down beneath trees decked with festoons of flowers. The residents of Badwell Ash in Suffolk were treated to tea and endless games and sport as their celebrations unfolded.

But in a newly commercial world, even these celebrations provided business opportunities. Weeks after the Jubilee, the *West Somerset Free Press* carried an advert by a photographer who had captured the festivities in Willerton, Old Cleeve and Dunster for posterity and who was willing to share them as souvenirs for a small fee.

The communal celebrations continued beyond Jubilee day with Victoria heading to one of them herself when she enjoyed a visit to the Children's Party in Hyde Park. Over 30,000 children were entertained to tea and games in an enormous operation that saw them organised into brigades and marshalled with military precision. The Queen seemed most impressed with the set-up and even happier with the news that each child would go home with an earthenware pot bearing her image. However, she was less won over by their musical prowess, writing in her journal that they *'sang God Save the Queen, somewhat out of tune'*.

On her way back to Windsor from this excursion, Victoria would get a taste of another celebratory tradition – the Jubilee arch. A few of these dramatic decorations had been put up in 1809 for her grandfather's festivities but they came into their own for the Golden

Jubilee of 1887. Truro in Cornwall boasted a collection in its ancient streets, including one which read 'Our Jubilee Greeting' and another declaring 'Victoria, Empress'. In Dalton in Cumbria, the arch was illuminated and featured the Queen's initials and her dates. The example in Loughton, Essex was widely praised, even if one critic pointed out that several of its letters were slightly wonky.

As she left London, Victoria passed through Eton where she stopped briefly at the decorative arch which was surrounded by yet more school children. However, their more expensive education had paid dividends for their singing was deemed to be far more in tune. From there, the Queen passed on to the centre of Windsor where her carriage stopped in front of a brand new statue of her which was about to be officially unveiled. It was one of hundreds of permanent tributes built around her kingdoms to mark her Jubilee.

In the first week of 1887 alone, dozens of plinths were laid for Jubilee statues and clock towers. Among them was the foundation of a clock tower at Brighton, the place where Victoria's uncle had spent so prodigiously and tipped his Monarchy into further debt and derision. Decades on from his reign, which had left royal popularity in tatters, the niece who had unexpectedly inherited his throne was being celebrated after a long reign which had helped rebuild the Crown. Furthermore, people were willingly dipping their hands into their pockets to pay for the privilege. The debauched days of George IV and his endless spending were long gone.

Across her realms, Victoria was celebrated in art and monuments with windows and clocks becoming particularly popular commemorations of the anniversary, being relatively easy to fund and house. By April 1887, Newbury in Berkshire had two subscriptions on the go, one for a clock to appear on Broadway in the town and another for a Jubilee window at the parish church. A Jubilee clock in Gravesend quickly became a landmark while the chapel of the City of London workhouse in Clapton was decorated with a new stained glass window marking Victoria's anniversary.

These local mementoes became staging posts in her reign, but her Jubilee had also seen reflection on the many changes that had taken place since she became Queen. The Manchester Royal Jubilee Exhibition opened in the month before Jubilee day aiming to showcase the many developments in art and manufacturing. Alongside paintings and sculpture were steam engines and demonstrations of mechanical processes like hat making while visitors were also entertained by Jubilee bands and fireworks. It proved hugely popular. Over 70,000 attended on Jubilee day itself with more than 4.7 million entrances across the whole five months of the exhibition.

The ongoing popularity of the show underlined the lasting impression this second royal Jubilee had made. Even the Queen seemed endlessly enamoured with it, commissioning several portraits of 'my Jubilee'. She called on the renowned military painter, John Charlton, to depict the parade through London. One of his interpretations emphasised the grandeur of the event and her central role in it. The Queen's carriage is shown at the heart of the huge parade, in the midst of cheering crowds at Trafalgar Square, with the lions around Nelson's Column framed by the red, white and blue of Union Jack bunting. It is the very image of power and all of it is centred on Victoria. She paid handsomely for the painting and handsomely for the celebrations. The government's refusal to bankroll the party led to the Queen footing the vast majority of the estimated costs as she stumped up around £50,000, but both realised the investment had been worthwhile.

The event had consolidated Britain's image as a leading world power. The soft diplomacy of dazzling so many European leaders with glittering Jubilee celebrations had created a base for expanding economic and social links. Victoria's family prestige had rocketed and the dynasty that she had formed with her much missed Albert was being feted around the world. The government's initial reluctance to pay for the Jubilee was replaced, as 1887 came to an end, with a realisation that it had actually done quite a lot to boost Britain's coffers.

Victoria would thank her people for their *'wonderful and so universal enthusiasm'* as the Jubilee itself ended and despite her reservations, and the frequent reference to the 'bothers' of organising the event, the Queen thoroughly enjoyed her Jubilee. Importantly, it had achieved its aims. There was concern that Victoria's general dislike of public appearances and her ongoing mourning for her husband had created a distance between her and her people, but the celebrations of 1887 had placed her at the heart of national life and she would remain there for the rest of her historic reign.

As 1887 came to an end, she noted in her journal that her daughter, Beatrice, had been the first to wish her a happy new year but *'it was with great regret I parted with the old eventful one. The Jubilee time was so richly blessed, not one mishap or disturbance, not one bad day...never can I forget this brilliant year.'*

Her Jubilee inkstand was looking a little worn by then. But, so too were the cynical remarks that had heralded her Jubilee. *The Globe* had noted on 1 January 1887 that when the Jubilee *'is over, we shall all probably feel thankful for one reason that we are never likely to see another Jubilee year'*.

They would soon run into disappointment. The golden celebrations had proved so successful that the chance to repeat the events before the century was over were too good to resist. All Victoria needed to do was keep on reigning for already plans were shaping up to fete her as no Monarch had been feted before. The most sparkling celebration of all was about to take place.

## Chapter Three

# Queen Victoria's Diamond Jubilee

Queen Victoria was in no doubt about the significance of the celebrations planned for the sixtieth anniversary of her accession. She would be the first Monarch in British history to reach this milestone and the first Sovereign in history to be given a Jubilee to mark it. Millions would join her festivities around the world and millions more would lap up every detail as the ever expanding press sent the story global. But for the woman who would star in the show, there was one more meaning to be taken from the events of 1897 – for Victoria herself, this was her swan song.

Not that there was anything of faded glory about the Queen or the festivities. Victoria was ten years older than at her previous Jubilee but the past decade had also seen her become a more familiar figure to her people and acquire an image as a kind and rather majestic matriarch to an empire. On the first day of her latest Jubilee year, the *Pall Mall Gazette* bemoaned the fact that the multitude of anniversary celebrations might mean the Queen appeared less at other events. Victoria went into her second Jubilee with the affection of her people secured.

Her health had deteriorated in the intervening years. Like her grandfather, George III, as he approached his Jubilee, Victoria now suffered sight problems, but the Queen, now in her late seventies, remained as determined and focused as ever. That combination of stubbornness and seniority would turn her second Jubilee into a success to rival her unexpectedly triumphant first.

There was much more of a fizz of excitement in the run up to this celebration than at the past two Jubilees of the nineteenth century.

For a start, more people understood what was about to happen. The Golden celebrations of 1887 were a recent memory for many meaning the vagueness of George III's festivities, when no one was really sure what a Jubilee was all about until it happened, and the tentativeness approaching Victoria's own half century were forgotten.

There was a template to follow and precedents had been set. Organisers knew what they should and shouldn't do as they designed set piece events. Local authorities understood how to marshal plans for parties and proposals to build clock towers, while revellers understood there would likely be a day off work and a chance to celebrate. Meanwhile, shopkeepers and business owners had their own understanding of what worked when it came to making money from the Monarchy. Victoria and her empire were ready for their Jubilee close-up.

However, just as in 1887, it would be the Queen who set the initial pace. Politicians had been pleasantly surprised at just how well her first Jubilee had gone and they wanted to maximise that success the second time round. Victoria was content to listen but was ready with her own ideas of how this event should unfold.

Firstly, a decision had to be taken on what to call the celebrations. Technically, a Jubilee was a period of fifty years, as set out in the Bible. However, that hadn't stopped the Papacy, which had first incorporated the celebration into western life, changing the numbers to suit the occasion. Popes now marked quarter centuries as Jubilees and, in the last decades of the nineteenth century, several European rulers had marked what were described by Victoria as their '25 Jubilee', taking their own quarter century as a milestone. However no other secular monarch had marked six decades of rule so describing this celebration was problematic – 60 Jubilee didn't have much of a ring to it. One grand suggestion was 'Jubilissimee' but that never gained much support.

It was Victoria's Private Secretary, Arthur Bigge, who was credited with finding the solution. Following the pattern of wedding anniversaries, especially popular on the continent, he suggested that June 1897 should be the Diamond Jubilee of the Queen.

There were other precedents that may have had an influence however. Jubilees had been part of the Catholic Church for centuries and, as life expectancy increased, more priests began to reach significant anniversaries. At the end of the nineteenth century there were increasing reports in the press of clerics marking Diamond Jubilees of their ordination or communion. The phrase wasn't unheard of when Bigge first coined it for the Queen, but the private secretary knew his Queen. Victoria was always prone to be contrary when her officials first made Jubilee suggestions. He presented his idea with the caveat that he understood the Queen wouldn't like it, thus increasing his chances of royal acceptance. Besides, like everyone, he knew Victoria remained eternally devoted to the memory of her late husband, Prince Albert. By bringing in wedding analogy, he added a reminder of the anniversaries she might have had with her much missed consort. The significance wasn't lost on either of them.

Victoria had never marked a '25 Jubilee', or Silver in wedding terminology, but that anniversary had fallen in June 1862, just six months after Albert's untimely death. Even if she had considered one, her widowhood would have made it impossible, but Victoria's later Jubilees indicated that she liked to plan in advance. There had been no mention of a celebration before Albert's death in December 1861 and both her Golden and Diamond celebrations were being talked about by the Queen over a year before they took place. Furthermore, in 1856, she had even taken the time to explain in her journals what a Jubilee was, having just spent time with a cleric who had marked his own. As the quarter century of her rule approached, Victoria gave little indication that it was something she planned to mark.

However, one remark in her journals indicates that a Silver celebration might have crossed her mind and, more importantly for the Queen, that of Albert. In 1869, Victoria makes her first mention of the '25 Jubilee'. She notes that the ruler celebrating is 'Ernest Coburg'.

That rather rudimentary name was actually how Victoria described the Duke of Saxe-Coburg-Gotha, the older brother to whom Albert had remained devoted despite fraternal bickering. Ernest and Albert had shared many ideas and when he reached his '25 Jubilee', Victoria remarked it brought many sad sensations. There is a possibility that Ernest Coburg was enjoying the party that Victoria and Albert had planned for her.

Even if it was the wedding analogy that sold the concept to her, Victoria had enough of a sense of her own importance to keep her mind on the task in hand as her Diamond Jubilee approached. Age meant she had lost some of the fervour that had marked the months before her Golden celebrations. As she reached the fifty-ninth anniversary of her accession and began the sixtieth year of her reign, on 20 June 1896, she was at Balmoral, as she had been ten years earlier. But unlike the past decade, there was no mention of festivity for the day. Instead, a quiet and reflective Queen noted that *'I have lived to see my dear country and vast Empire prosper and expand and be wonderfully loyal.'*

It is almost a politician's response to the anniversary, the focus firmly on what should be said at such a momentous time with an awareness that, despite the personal nature of her diary now, at some point her words would become public property. But it also summed up the attitude to the Diamond Jubilee from the Queen and her advisers. Now, well aware of what the celebrations should be, the official response was centred on making that a reality. For, as with the past Jubilees, there was more than the Monarch to think about.

The idea of a popular festivity that placed the Sovereign at the heart of British life had found an audience far more willing than even the most ardent royalist could have hoped for. The local officials planning the Diamond celebrations were surrounded by reminders of the most recent Jubilee, walking to work in buildings that bore its name or that of the Queen or past fields loaned by generous owners for parties that still lingered in the collective memory. Committees were soon forming around Britain to manage Jubilee celebrations.

The main events were somewhat easier to plan in 1897. Government ministers were keen to repeat the spectacular success of the royal parade that had carried Victoria to Westminster Abbey in a scene that helped reinforce the image of her power. The Queen was happy to oblige, on three conditions. Firstly, this was not to be a state occasion, rather an official celebration. The delineation was important. Removing the trappings of state meant there was no pressure to invite the endless crowned heads of Europe who had peopled her Golden Jubilee. Despite being related to many of them, Victoria had no intention of bringing them to London for her 'swan song'. Her closest relations would be there but the continent's other kings and queens could send telegrams and wish her well from afar.

The decision removed one of the main obstacles to a glorious Jubilee. In the past decade, the Queen's eldest grandchild, Wilhelm, had become, firstly, Kaiser of Prussia and, subsequently, a thorn in the side of several European powers. His brusque, bullying style of diplomacy caused waves as did his aggressive policies. His grandmama had had enough and wanted no part of him at her party.

Removing royalty from the celebration also meant there was less pressure for Victoria to pay for the festivities herself. In 1887 the throngs of relations who joined her Jubilee had been one of the reasons her government was able to pass the majority of the rather substantial bills her way. The Queen had ended up over £50,000 out of pocket in a celebration that had benefitted her politicians as much as her. She had no intention of paying up again in 1897. Either the government covered the costs or Victoria wasn't taking part. The Queen was once again triumphant.

Her third and final condition was seemingly the most simple but also among the most problematic. Now riddled with arthritis and finding it increasingly hard to move, Victoria decreed that she was happy to sit in a carriage and parade among her people as they cheered her on Jubilee day. However, she would not get out of her landau at any point. In 1887 she had witnessed several important celebratory moments from her carriage, including the unveiling of a statue in the heart of Windsor, but she had left its confines to walk into Westminster Abbey for the high point of the festivities, the Service of Thanksgiving for her reign. This time round, she would not be moved. The Jubilee would have to be built around her, quite literally.

A solution was quickly found. As with past Jubilees, a church service giving thanks for the long life and reign of the Monarch was an absolute necessity. However, given Victoria's infirmity it was agreed that her carriage would take her as far as the steps of St. Paul's Cathedral and then the church would come to her. It would prove to be a masterstroke for it set Victoria, very visibly, at the heart of a show of power and prestige.

However, that much anticipated and highly coveted image of British superiority was under threat from another of her conditions, her moratorium on other monarchs. The adulatory crowds needed some world leaders among them to make them truly potent. And the political success of the Golden Jubilee had come from showing other countries first hand just how well Victoria's realms were doing. Politicians were in dire need of powerful people to show off to for this Jubilee.

In the end, Empire provided the solution. The Colonial Secretary, Joseph Chamberlain, suggested inviting the premiers of all of Britain's self-governing colonies to the celebrations. They accepted and promised to bring military escorts which would only add to the splendour of the planned procession. Chamberlain also persuaded them to join him in a conference in London where, for the first time, the political leaders of all Victoria's governments could meet face to face. This round dozen of men would come together to discuss issues affecting millions of people across the world who were all under the ultimate rule of one woman. It was an impressive and ambitious result. The second Jubilee of Victoria had been transformed into a Festival of British Empire and a stunning show of her imperial realms, that vast expanse on which the sun never set.

Despite the intended glory, all those watching would have to take the Queen as they found her. Just as with her Golden celebrations, Victoria had no intention of dressing the part of all-powerful empress. The idea of her wearing her crown and Robe of State was briefly floated but no one really expected her to acquiesce. Victoria would wear black, as usual, and a bonnet with a trim of lace and a few jewels.

Instead, the embodiment of the Queen as a regal figure would be saved for the multitude of statues, busts and commemorations that once more began to spring to life around her country as her latest Jubilee approached. In Brighton, the planned statue was shared in the local press and displayed Victoria in a long gown, covered with a sash, and wearing a crown. The Jubilee statue erected in Dundee for the Diamond celebrations showed the Queen seated, again in a glorious long dress with a crown on top of her erect head, and holding the orb and sceptre.

Like the monuments of the Golden Jubilee, these public records of the sixtieth anniversary of the Queen's reign added all the regal elements she refused to indulge on the day itself. Even her own daughter had chosen to represent her in an idealised rather than realistic fashion. Princess Louise, Duchess of Argyll had designed the statue which had been commissioned for outside Kensington Palace for her mother's first Jubilee and which had finally been erected in 1893. At the creative direction of her daughter, the ageing monarch had been transformed into her young self, holding the symbols of her majesty and gazing out at the capital of her Empire.

The multitude of souvenirs that began to pour into shops were the same. Victoria was nearly always shown with her small crown atop her head and a little lace veil at the back. On Jubilee beakers and plates, she remained the image of majesty and, this time round, was shown more often with younger representations of herself, again always crowned. The mementoes of her Jubilee had very little to do with the woman being celebrated and everything to do with what she represented.

Victoria herself understood that well. And although she wasn't prepared to dress up for the Diamond Jubilee, she did ensure that the main image of her shared throughout the celebrations matched the idealised version. She took the rare step of releasing a photograph of herself, with no copyright conditions attached. It meant that anyone, from the leading jewellers of the day to the lowliest shopkeeper, could use it without charge – and they did. Victoria chose how she would be represented at this first ever Diamond Jubilee in a masterstroke of PR manipulation.

The image showed her in black, as always, but much of her mourning gown is trimmed in white lace. She wears a tiny, diamond crown and the diamond necklace chosen for her Coronation. She sits, side on, looking into the distance. Her hands clutch a white fan which points discreetly to her Order of the Garter Star, a reminder of her role at the very heart of the ancient institution of Monarchy. And on show at the centre of the image is her wedding ring, her most precious gift from Albert.

It was the very image of royalty and became the very image of her Jubilee, but it was as representative of the Queen at the time of her Jubilee as the glorious statues for this was an old photograph. Victoria hadn't posed for posterity in the year of her celebration. She had selected a picture taken several years earlier, for the marriage of her grandson, George, and Mary of Teck. Victoria wanted to be seen in her prime. The jubilee was about an idealised version of Monarchy and the Queen had found the picture perfect representation of that.

She was less accommodating with other aspects of her celebration. The actual anniversary of her accession, 20 June, fell on a Sunday and it was felt inappropriate to mark the event on the sabbath. Instead, it was suggested that the following day might be useful but Victoria preferred the Tuesday and so the date was set for 22 June 1897.

Before then the Queen passed another milestone and one that excited almost as much comment as her Jubilees, even if she had been equally insistent that no great celebration take place to mark it. In September 1896 she became Britain's longest reigning Monarch. George III had ruled for 59 years and 3 months. His granddaughter passed that mark on 23 September 1896 to great fanfare. Her record breaking achievement made the front of many newspapers around the world while so many congratulatory telegrams were received at Balmoral, where Victoria was holidaying in the company of the Tsar of Russia, that a special team of five operators had to be employed for the day to deal with them.

A service of thanksgiving was held at Holy Trinity Church, Windsor where the Dean remarked that 'she was Queen, not only of the Empire, but also of the hearts of her people' while the bells rang out at St. Margaret's Church, Westminster and the royal standard was hoisted at St. Martin's in the Field. Victoria requested there be no gun salutes on the historic day or any public recognition of it but she did send a telegram to the Mayor of London which was displayed outside the Mansion House for the capital to read.

*The London Illustrated News* noted the official rejection of a Jubilee celebration for her milestone, adding '*it would, to some minds, have seemed inappropriate, almost invidious, to appoint a formal public celebration in September 1896 of the bare fact that Her Majesty Queen Victoria had reigned a day longer than her grandfather, George III*'. But it marked the day with pages of praise-filled words and more historic images. For the pictures it chose were of Victoria with her eldest son, Edward, his own son, George, and the firstborn of that prince, another Edward. As Victoria approached her Diamond celebrations, she wasn't just a Jubilee Queen. She was the mother of an empire and the matriarch of a dynasty that would rule that imperial realm well into the next century.

Many papers chose to contrast this record breaking ruler with the young Queen who had taken the throne as a teenager in 1837.

Then, the Monarchy had been in a precarious situation. Now, wrote editorials across the land, the Crown was stronger than ever before and the many changes overseen by Victoria, hailed as the epitome of a constitutional monarch, had transformed Britain into the envy of the world and ruler of half the globe.

*The Toronto Saturday Night* stated with confidence that *'there is probably no living person who exercises a greater influence in European politics than does the Queen and this despite the fact that never in the slightest degree through her long reign has she acted in other than a strictly constitutional manner'.*

Meanwhile, some papers, like the *Falkirk Herald*, were so swept up by the string of royal achievements that they declared Victoria was actually the longest reigning European monarch, as the real record holder, Louis XIV, had succeeded as a child and spent far too many years of his youth under a regency to allow him to claim a personal rule to compete with Victoria.

The celebration of Victoria's record only heightened anticipation of her forthcoming Jubilee. As the Lord Mayor of London sent a congratulatory message and Madame Tussauds put on a special exhibition to mark her record-breaking achievement, others were discussing how they would really party when they were finally allowed to in June 1897.

*The Weymouth Telegram* reported the gushing words of the Mayor as he told a council meeting '*Victoria, our Queen and Empress, is honoured and respected in every country and at the celebration of the sixtieth year of her reign, which will take place next year, I am sure the wish of every English heart will be the same as that which found so mighty and universal utterance 60 years ago, when the prayer of her people at her coronation was "long may she reign".*'

Meanwhile, the Victoria Hospital for Children in London was already advertising its 'grand imperial fete and fancy fair' to mark the sixtieth anniversary of the queen's accession, promising free tickets for children on one of its four days of celebrations, with over 300 applications received nine months before it even opened.

Around the country, Jubilee tributes were already under construction. A new reading room in Runcorn was attracting subscriptions as autumn gave way to winter, while in the run up to Christmas the foundation stone for an extension of the Jubilee alms houses at Greenwich was laid, providing further accommodation to that built to mark the anniversary celebrations of 1809 and 1887.

A popular focus for fundraising to mark Victoria's Diamond festivities was her Jubilee Institute for Nurses. It had been established after the Queen gave it a grant of £70,000 from the Women's Jubilee Fund in 1887 with the aim of training and supporting nurses to look after the poor. In an echo of the Jubilee notion of helping those most in need, it became a beneficiary of many local campaigns that sprang up ahead of the anniversary celebrations.

As the great year got under way, the *Pall Mall Gazette* noted that '*the unique occasion will be celebrated in so many ways that if it were not that the enthusiasm of the promoters of rival schemes of commemoration is so laudable, we might be disposed to deprecate the multiplicity of them.*'

Meanwhile, *The Times* on 1 January 1897 was effusive in its anticipation, writing *'whatever fortune the year upon which we enter today may bring the British Empire, it will remain ever memorable in our annals, as that of the solemn celebration of the "diamond jubilee" of Queen Victoria'*, before adding, a little ominously, '*if, as we all trust, Her Majesty is spared to us'*.

Victoria was feeling equally sanguine about the forthcoming celebrations, noting in her diary '*may the year be one of peace…may I yet be spared some years in health and strength and possession of my intellect, so as to be of use to my country.*'

As the planning continued, there were fewer mentions of 'my Jubilee' in Victoria's journals in comparison to the months ahead of her Golden celebrations and the references were usually much more curt, often just referring to conversations in which events had been discussed with no details of what was being debated. In part, this was down to her diminished role in the planning and her determination to exclude many of her royal relations from the event. The government was marshalling this into a celebration of Empire while on a local level, the now well oiled machinery of communal celebration was preparing parties and tailoring tributes in a most efficient fashion. The Queen could rise above it all and she did.

Victoria even found time to go on holiday in the months before her Diamond celebrations. In March 1897 she travelled to the south of France with some of her closest family but even on her way to Cimiez, she couldn't escape the great event. Her journal notes that on landing at Cherbourg she was presented with a 'congratulatory address' for the Jubilee, signed by the British residents in the surrounding area.

Her stay in France would be marked by a household row over Abdul Karim, the Indian servant who had been brought to Windsor for the Golden Jubilee and who had since become a close confidante of the Queen. Victoria returned to England with her household intact and plans for her latest celebrations on track.

She turned more to her family for support, noting in May 1897 that her heir, the Prince of Wales, had been '*kind and helpful*' about some '*arrangements for the Jubilee which are rather alarming*' while a cryptic entry just days before the celebrations describes *'the trouble about arranging things for the Jubilee still continues'*. But the references to Jubilee in her journals remain business-like and to the point. The personal input and passion of the first festivities has been replaced by pure professionalism.

In early June, she records that she spent some time with her third daughter, Louise, trying to arrange the princes who she had permitted to be present into some kind of precedence. It would prove a painful exercise and not just because of protocol. Since her last Jubilee, the line to her throne and the happiness of her family had been disrupted by the deaths of four men who had ridden by her carriage for her

Golden Jubilee. As she arranged the HRHs attending her latest celebration, she was reminded of all that was now gone.

Three of her five sons-in-law had died in the intervening decade while the loss of her grandson, Albert Victor, had shaken the succession. The prince was the eldest son of Victoria's heir, Edward, Prince of Wales, and since his birth in 1864, had been a guarantee of his dynasty. His role had been quickly taken by his brother, George, who had even gone on to marry Albert Victor's fiancée, but as Victoria wrote the names of her royal relations in order for the Diamond Jubilee, the missing prince was a reminder of all that had changed and how much pain that had brought on a personal level.

She was thinking of those she had lost when the sixtieth anniversary of her reign finally arrived. Victoria spent the day at Windsor where she attended a special service at St. George's Chapel. Just as had happened on the fiftieth anniversary of her reign, she heard Prince Albert's Te Deum while a newly composed Jubilee hymn, with music by Arthur Sullivan and words by the Bishop of Wakefield, was also sung. But Victoria's mind was firmly in the past, as she wrote in her journal:

> 'I was much touched and overcome, especially when all my children and grandchildren came up to me and kissed me and I kissed them, just as I did 10 years ago at Westminster Abbey. How many of my dear ones have gone since then!'

Just as there had been during her Golden celebrations, there were presents. Her offspring clubbed together to present her with a diamond sautoir chain but as with many things produced in 1897, it had a Jubilee novelty attached to it. The clasp of this royal present was made of the dates of the start of Victoria's reign and her Diamond Jubilee as well as a crown. Victoria doesn't reveal if she put it on before heading off for her most solemn duty of the day, laying a wreath at the tomb of her beloved Albert.

It was to be her last moment of calm for some days. On the morning of 21 June 1897, Victoria travelled by train to London where the quiet of the mausoleum was replaced by the instant roar of the crowds. Massive turnouts were waiting for their Jubilee Queen – it was estimated that around three million people visited London in the days of the Diamond celebrations. They packed the short route from Paddington Station to Buckingham Palace. Despite the crowds and her failing eyesight, Victoria enjoyed the glory of the Jubilee decorations and was particularly impressed with one arch going across Cambridge Terrace which read 'Our hearts thy Throne'. She was cheered through Hyde Park Corner and along Constitution Hill by an ever-growing throng. Once inside Buckingham Palace, a few minutes rest was scheduled before more festivities took over.

She was allowed a brief lunch before heading off to the Bow Room to greet more family as well as foreign dignitaries. It was an impressive line up and a much more relaxed one without the presence of Victoria's grandson, Kaiser Wilhelm, who she had always intended to exclude from her party.

This was a day of history at the start of a spectacle that was intended to show Britain's power to the world. In a strange twist of fate, the first foreign royal presented to Victoria was a man who would unwittingly put that power to the test within a few years. As Victoria was wheeled into position to greet her guests, the first to walk forward to pay homage was Archduke Franz Ferdinand whose assassination in 1914 would send the Empire now being feted to war with the forces of the absent Kaiser.

The power show continued with the presentation of an endless string of foreign dignitaries with the Queen shaking hands and receiving visitors for several hours. Even in private, the work continued as Victoria was regaled with telegrams. But by the evening, she was ready for another display of potency as the Queen put on a black dress with an imperial twist. The front had been worked in gold embroidery in India. The Diamond Queen added diamonds to her cap and her neck and progressed into a dining room filled with her foreign guests. Queen Victoria was back to her best, exercising her soft diplomacy and setting this Jubilee off with a sparkle.

While many of the 25,000 troops who would form the procession slept in makeshift tents in Hyde Park and stable boys polished the landaus that would convey the royal family through the streets of London, Victoria slept in her least favourite home despite the noise for revellers had taken over the streets of her capital for a party a decade in the making.

This Jubilee shared many things with its predecessors. Both had seen popular partying and a huge groundswell of support for the Monarchy, but the Diamond celebrations were different, too. They were the first to be filmed on a grand scale, with early newsreel cameras capturing the processions and they attracted a more intense media interest around the world. Among those covering the event was the American writer, Mark Twain.

Twain was already in the capital when he was asked by William Randolph Hearst to write about the Jubilee for the *San Francisco Examiner*. Whether he had already arranged it or whether his eager commissioning editor sorted it out, Twain found himself in one of the highly sought after seats in the stands that had been built along the Strand. Places on the procession route had been selling fast for months while windows and balconies along the six mile journey were crammed with spectators. The sheer body of people who had come to see the Queen made a massive impression on Twain as did the military parade. By the time tiny Victoria in her black dress approached, he was already quite overcome by the spectacle.

The show was designed to cement Britain as the leading imperial power of the world and it contained all the elements of nineteenth century military might to do it. Troops from across the Empire, from Canada, Australia, the South Pacific and India rode alongside the British Army and Navy in a parade of thousands designed to impress millions. The Queen's carriage had an escort of Life Guards and Indian officers and Victoria sat alone, with the Princess of Wales and Princess Louise opposite her. Her very loneliness became hugely symbolic for Twain who described the crowd standing, as one, as Victoria approached, adding '*all the rest of it was mere embroidery.... in her, the public saw the British Empire itself*'.

Victoria was quite overcome with the reception given to her as well. She was amazed by the size of the crowds lining Constitution Hill and touched to see the Chelsea Pensioners waiting there for her. The numbers swelled as she approached Piccadilly and the Strand and the approach to the City of London where the crowds were treated to an ancient tradition as the Lord Mayor presented the sword to his Monarch and, having seen her touch its hilt, swung it above his head and rode off in front of her. The numbers of well-wishers were so large as Victoria finally approached St. Paul's that her carriage stopped several times as the national anthem broke out. But there was more emotion as she realised that among those come to see her were the survivors of the Charge of the Light Brigade at Balaclava who were gathered in a house near to the Cathedral.

The decision to hold the Service of Thanksgiving at St. Paul's had been taken because its steps provided the perfect setting for a celebration centred around Victoria's carriage. As she pulled up the clergy were already in position, led by the Archbishop of Canterbury and the Bishop of London. They had put on their finest copes for the event but Victoria had surprised no one by dressing entirely in black. However, around her carriage stood all her royal princes in their finery. It was a living embodiment of majesty and all paid homage to the Jubilee Queen at its centre.

The outdoor service was short. A specially composed Te Deum, the work of a Doctor Martin, was sung and the Lord's Prayer was said followed by a special Jubilee prayer and the singing of the 'Old 100th', better known now as 'All People who on Earth Do Dwell'. The blessing ended the service along with the National Anthem and, after a brief audience with her clerics, Victoria was on her way into the throng again with the Archbishop of Canterbury sending her on her way by raising three cheers for his Queen.

The royal route back to Buckingham Palace took in the Mansion House where the Lady Mayoress handed over a silver basket of orchids before a moment of military might saw the Queen's carriage go over London Bridge with only troops for company. It was the one part of the route barred to spectators.

The crowds had gathered in force again as the Queen arrived in Borough Road, the poorest area on her Jubilee parade route. Victoria's journal showed she was moved by the effort that had been made to fete her, describing the floral garlands which hung along the streets. She then continued to Westminster Bridge, past Parliament and through Whitehall before heading to Horse Guards and the Mall. Back at the Palace, Victoria retired to take lunch although the sound of her military parade kept her company as the troops continued their procession back to base while the Jubilee Queen rested.

A regal dinner and ball followed with the Queen wearing her Jubilee necklace and a brooch given to her by her household along with a black dress decked with silver. She retired to try and sleep through another hot night while in the streets outside, thousands feted her. She needed her rest for Victoria's second Jubilee was about to present another innovation. In 1809, the party was done by the end of the Jubilee day itself, while in 1887 the official celebrations trailed off delicately once the anniversary had been and gone. Now, the seventy-eight-year-old Queen was lined up to take centre stage in a string of events that would take her Jubilee celebrations into July.

It all started on 23 June at Buckingham Palace. An integral part of the homage paid to the Monarchy at the first Jubilee had been the loyal addresses of cities, towns and villages across George III's kingdom. That tradition was now amplified as a tired queen sat in a baking hot room at her hated London home to be feted by the great and the good of her Empire. First came the Lords, all walking towards the Queen who sat on a dais in the ballroom with the Prince and

Princess of Wales behind her. They read a loyal address to which she gave a brief reply before the Commons entered to repeat the homage.

Next on the list of those who wanted to praise their Queen were the chairmen of County Councils followed by 400 mayors and provosts. Victoria sat, listening and smiling, nodding and acknowledging as the tributes poured in. She finally left the Palace but the addresses weren't over. After inspecting the Yeoman of the Guard, her carriage took her along Constitution Hill for more tributes.

At George III's Jubilee, the leading universities of his realm had sent addresses. That tradition continued but Victoria's second celebrations expanded it further. She had made her way through massive crowds with 10,000 children given prime spots in the stands. As her carriage stopped near Hyde Park Corner, loyal addresses were made by the School Board, the Church and representatives of the Catholic, Jewish and Wesleyan schools as well as non-denominational schools. It was a modern and inclusive move. At the time of George III's Jubilee, emancipation for Catholic and Jewish communities was still years away. As his granddaughter ended the century with another royal celebration, those faiths were given a central role in her festivities.

Victoria and her Royal Family showed their PR savvy at this round of tributes, too. Seated in a carriage was Prince Edward, known to his family as David, the toddler great grandson who was in direct line to inherit the imperial throne now being feted. David sat in a carriage with his father, George, second in line while nearby was his grandfather, the Prince of Wales. As Victoria went among this youthful and diverse gathering of her people at the official Jubilee celebrations, she was surrounded by her three kings in waiting. It was a powerful image of the Queen, her dynasty and all her people.

Meanwhile, at another stop on her journey away from London, the Queen was greeted by a stand of nurses, in their white caps and uniforms, a reminder of the growing range of work available to women, six decades into the rule of Britain's Queen.

As Victoria left London, her role at the heart of Empire was underlined further as masses of colonial troops waited for her at Paddington to cheer her train off as it departed the capital. It stopped at Slough where she was presented with more loyal addresses as well as flowers handed over by a group of orphans. With another escort of colonial troops, she made her way through the town underneath Jubilee arches. Another arch greeted the Queen at Eton but this was more dramatic, containing school pupils perched precariously above the streets to act as heralds. The loyal address of the school was the last of the day. Around half past seven on this midsummer's evening, the Queen was allowed to make her way to Windsor Castle. She ate quickly and retired.

But the decorated streets had made an impression. Victoria was desperate to get out and see them again but it took her until early evening the following day as she found herself confronted with an assembly of admirals along with their captains, all of whom were presented to her as eager participants in an upcoming naval review. When she did start out on her latest carriage ride, she found the crowds around Windsor just as big as the previous days. A carnival had just come to an end and its participants surged around her carriage, in their costumes, much to the Queen's delight. As she made her way back up Castle Hill, the crowds began to shower her with confetti. The wedding analogy of the Diamond Jubilee was complete.

However, the Jubilee celebrations were not, so on 25 June 1897 Victoria set off for a children's party in a field outside Windsor where 6,000 eager youngsters were ready to greet her. From there, she graced the Jubilee party of the Fire Brigades from across England which was being held nearby. On her return to the castle there were yet more festivities waiting for her as Eton College had arrived for a torchlight procession and songs. The performance obviously impressed the Queen who declared it gave her 'much pleasure'.

She seemed to gain a similar feeling from the events of the following day. Several members of her family were dispatched to a naval review while Victoria stayed at Windsor. As well as a very long ceremony, they were deluged in a huge thunderstorm and returned home late. The Queen's glee in missing the misery was almost palpable.

The programme was easily the most intense of any of the three anniversary celebrations of the nineteenth century. She was back in London on 28 June where she planted a tree in Kensington after listening to more loyal addresses and then hosted a Jubilee garden party at Buckingham Palace attended by leading lights including Ellen Terry. Victoria made it back to Windsor that night and the following day, a full week on from the first of her Jubilee celebrations, she found herself inspecting a parade of 4,000 volunteers from thirty-three public schools. The next morning brought loyal addresses from across Windsor while 1 July saw the Queen at Aldershot for a military review.

Celebrations began to draw to an end with a review of the colonial troops who had come to England for her Jubilee. But as Victoria bade them farewell, on 2 July 1897, she told their commanding officer *'will you tell...the men what a great pleasure it has been to me to see so many of my subjects...I hope they will all return here some day and I wish them happiness and all prosperity.'*

There was a garden party at Windsor the next day, 3 July, for members of the House of Commons and the Queen's keen sense of politics was on show. She recorded in her diary that *'some of the (so called) Labour members were presented, which I heard afterwards gratified them very much'*. A further spring was put in her step by the arrival of the Archbishop of Finland for dinner with Victoria dedicating the best part of a page of her diary to his looks, personality and charm.

The tired, sad Queen of the start of June had been transformed into an energetic, enthusiastic monarch by the success of her latest Jubilee, her so called 'swan song'. But this wasn't just Victoria's swan song. It was the final curtain for the idealised version of old Britain where the rich offered their patronage to the poor at special times with food, drink and sport, a brief moment of gratitude for years of hard work.

That beneficence began at the very top. Over 300,000 of London's poorest inhabitants were provided with a party through a fund set up by the hugely popular Princess of Wales. She had invited public contributions to provide a Jubilee repast and, in another nod to the major changes of the nineteenth century, found her feast facilitated by large scale sponsorship. The tea magnate, Thomas Lipton, donated over £25,000 while the Australian meat industry sent 20,000 carcasses to turn into a meal fit for a Queen's Jubilee.

The old ideal of the wealthy caring for the poor was brought to vivid life by the Princess who visited several of the celebrations, taking food to the poor and listening to their stories. The *Daily Telegraph and Courier* turned it into an embodiment of aspiration, noting that she went from table to table, *'with a kindly word for the maimed and the cripples and the little children, so wonderful an apparition must have seemed part of dreamland – the advent of a fairy, able to touch with the wand of her gentle kindliness, the mean and common lives of the poor and transform them into a radiant scene of happiness'*.

In Edinburgh, the poor and needy were invited to a huge feast at Waverley Market where they listened to a speech from the Lord Provost before falling upon the 'pies and tarts' laid on for their supper. Around them stood the great and good of the city, the High Constables, the military and the ministers of the church.

In Alcombe in Somerset, a feast for residents of the village was put on followed by an afternoon of sports. The inhabitants had paraded through flag-decked streets for the opening of their new reading room, the Victoria, while the ambitious landlord of the New Inn had erected an arch for the event bearing the slogan 'The Quantock Hills resounded with cheers, telling love of sixty years.'

In Blankney in Lincolnshire, the generous Mr. Hunt threw open the doors of his barn for all the adults in the area to enjoy a 'knife and fork tea', while the streets were hung with flags and streamers and a Jubilee arch appeared, bearing the dates of Victoria's reign. Mr Raymond Lewis won great praise in Sapperton, Gloucestershire for opening up Manor Farm buildings to host a tea for local children and a dinner for their adults, all paid for by subscription, while in North Nibley, Lord Fitzharding was widely noted as the generous founder of the local Jubilee feast. It was a rural idyll brought to life, a representation of the Victorian ideal and it was repeated across the land.

Not everything was quite so perfect though. One Jubilee party at Prestwick led to a court case after the children sitting down to it were presented with 'sandwiches…alive with maggots, and the currant cake mouldy'. Suppliers keen to capitalise on Diamond fever had scooped up the remnants of an earlier party and held on to it until Jubilee day. Their party was so grim, the children refused to eat it. The case came to court in mid July, as Jubilee fervour finally began to fade.

However, it had made a lasting impression on millions. It would prove to be Victoria's swan song. Her reign lasted another three and a half years. She had taken the throne as the youthful hope of the Monarchy and ended it as a genial mother figure. No one writing her obituaries was in any doubt that her reign had saved the Crown and her Jubilees had played a large part in boosting its image.

As she had driven out on her Diamond Jubilee parade, Victoria had pressed a button which had sent an electronic telegram around her Empire. It read, simply '*From my heart, I thank my beloved people, may God bless them.*'

A dozen words, sent thousands of miles to millions of subjects, but that one message summed up the Jubilees that her royal house had instigated less than a century earlier. They had started off as a vague wish to consolidate the very concept of royalty by underlining its position at the heart of national life, but they had been transformed by the very people they were meant to impress. By the time of Victoria's

Diamond celebrations, popular understanding of what made a Jubilee informed the festivities and the royal response to them. The Queen was aware of a growing vision of the Sovereign as both ruler and servant of the people.

Victoria meant every one of those twelve words. The message was heartfelt, and it was filled with thanks and blessings. But, most of all, it was for those who had created the royal celebrations of Jubilee. The people.

# Chapter Four

# Reinventing the Jubilee for King George V

George V's reign had seen war, economic hardship and the fall of monarchies around Europe. Through it all, the King had maintained a calm resolve. He had never matched the charisma of his more exciting relatives, nor had he shown any inclination to try. George, for a large number of those living in his realms in 1935, was the safe, steady and sensible old King, yet, in many ways, he was an innovator and his Jubilee showed that. Behind the bunting decked façade of a traditional anniversary celebration were changes that brought the festivities into a new century without upsetting that sense of reassurance that the now established pattern of partying brought with it.

For a start, George was the first British monarch to mark a Silver Jubilee. The decision to celebrate the quarter century of his rule showed all the common sense he was known for. The King was, by 1935, approaching his seventieth birthday. Just a few years earlier, he had been seriously ill with septicaemia and for a while his doctors had feared for his life. The ever practical George would have been the first to admit he most likely wouldn't be around to celebrate the fiftieth anniversary of his reign. This was his one chance to use the power of a Jubilee.

Like George III and Victoria before him, this milestone in his reign came at a time when the Monarchy needed a boost. George had been a popular and successful King but many of the thrones which had been in place at the start of his reign had disappeared rapidly amidst war and social change. He had already done much to bolster his dynasty, including changing its name from Saxe-Coburg-Gotha to the very British sounding Windsor as anti-German sentiment reached its zenith during the First World War. He had stripped away many of his relatives' titles at the same time, in a regal clear-out that was meant to reset the Monarchy in British life. And he had maintained a man of the people image, conscious that the ostentatious trappings of royal life could be a barrier in a world recovering from a war which had led to revolutions and a financial crisis that was impacting on millions as his milestone anniversary approached. Throughout his reign, he had worked to shore up his throne in a new century rapidly tiring of the old institution of royalty. A jubilee would provide another opportunity to strengthen it further.

While the first royal Jubilees had marked half centuries of rule, the idea of a silver celebration for twenty-five years, in line with traditional wedding anniversaries, had gained currency in the past decades. In 1897, King Oskar II of Sweden had enjoyed a hugely successful celebration for his quarter century on the throne. George's own brother-in-law, King Haakon VII of Norway, had also marked a Silver Jubilee. In 1930, he had held celebrations in Oslo with a royal gala concert and banquet with guests including George's fourth son, the future Duke of Kent. However the festivities for Haakon and his wife, Queen Maud, had a less popular aspect to them, although the King of Norway issued a medal to mark his Jubilee. More in line with the public festivities that George V would mastermind in 1935 were the events held for Queen Wilhelmina of the Netherlands in 1923.

Wilhelmina chose to have a Jubilee when her personal rule reached a quarter of a century. She had taken the throne as a ten-year-old, in 1898, but her mother had ruled as regent for eight years. Wilhelmina marked her Jubilee for the part of her reign between 1898 and 1923. The complicated maths didn't put off her country which took the Jubilee celebrations very seriously. Public buildings were decorated with flags and banners, souvenirs were issued and the queen and her family processed through her capital to acclaim.

It was far more similar to the Jubilees that had marked Victoria's reign and George was determined to stick to this template of public celebration.

However, not everyone was convinced by this new adaptation. In many parts of Scotland, it was described as a 'semi-Jubilee'. The *Falkirk Herald* reminded its readers of the Biblical origin of a true Jubilee as marking fifty years, with an observation that King George V and Queen Mary had reached 'only a semi-jubilee'. However, George put his support behind the idea and he was already involved in plans to mark his twenty-fifth anniversary the year before it happened, taking a close interest in developments, and those preparations included subtle innovations to move this traditional celebration into a new century.

Jubilee beacons would be lit, with the King starting the chain, but instead of appearing in public with a flaming torch in hand, George would start this chain of fire by pressing an electric button which would ignite a beacon in Hyde Park. He was a keen philatelist and, despite reservations about the merit of any commemorative stamp, decided that it was too good an opportunity to miss and became particularly fussy over the appearance of his Jubilee edition. He also decided to bring his festivities into the heart of every home by broadcasting a Jubilee message.

George had already introduced the Christmas speech, first addressing the Empire by radio in 1932. While Victoria had issued Jubilee messages in written form, George would speak directly to his people on the evening of his great celebration, ending that day with an innovation that he hoped would become part of royal tradition. But despite the changes, the basic format of the Jubilee was to remain the same. There would be a Service of Thanksgiving, a carriage parade, loyal addresses and a balcony appearance. Illuminations, the bedrock of the first British royal Jubilee, would play a significant part, and, like past festivities, this would be a popular celebration. Feasting and games would be held while helping those most in need would remain fundamental to the celebrations. All the characteristics of past royal celebrations were present as the first British Silver Jubilee took shape.

George V, like the two Jubilee Monarchs in Britain's past, had come to the throne at a time of good weather. It was easy to fix his celebrations for the actual anniversary of his accession as spring would be at its height and 6 May 1935 was declared Jubilee Day and made a bank holiday. However, the build up began much earlier with 1935 called a Jubilee year from its earliest days.

The celebration also brought a first real wave of Jubilee tourism and a sharpened sense of commercial opportunity. Travel had become cheaper and easier in the time since Victoria's Diamond celebrations and there were plenty of people happy to exploit that. Excursions from Belfast to London were offered by Thomas Cook while newspapers in the capital became so concerned about the number of cars expected to drive into its streets to catch sight of the celebrations that several published daily articles in the run up to the festivities asking people to leave their vehicles at home.

The Jubilee became a focus for advertisers, too. Commercials appeared in newspapers offering new furniture in time for celebratory parties, while companies including Barnett's of Kensington offered royal themed novelties for dances and parties. A special souvenir Crown issued by the Royal Mint proved so popular that its 2,500 run was soon oversubscribed and eager collectors were confined to one example each with many missing out altogether.

A host of books appeared to mark the event while reviewers set out their favoured biographies of the Royal Family for those whose interest in the Windsors had been piqued by the Jubilee. George's determination to show his dynasty as a family may have helped mellow its image and increase its popularity, but it also led to an increased interest in their private lives. This was reflected in one recommendation in the *London Daily News* which advised '*those more interested in the human side of the Royal Family' to seek out a tome by Lady Cynthia Asquith called 'God Save the King!'*. Meanwhile,

Sir Philip Gibbs produced 'The Book of the King's Jubilee', packed with over 500 photos for the anniversary, another indication of how mass media had become more vital to this royal celebration than any before it.

But there were other, more serious changes to contend with. Those organising the festivities were acutely aware that almost four decades had passed since the last Jubilee and the realms being called on to celebrate were very different from those known by Victoria. Ireland was a case in point. In 1897 loyal addresses had been sent from Dublin, even if discontent with the Monarchy was felt across the wider population. George had become King of Ireland on his accession in 1910. However, that masked the reality of a deep-rooted desire among many for independence from Britain. The Irish Civil War was followed by partition in 1921 with six counties of Ulster remaining with the United Kingdom while the other twenty-six counties formed the Irish Free State. By the time George reached his Silver Jubilee, just Northern Ireland remained under his royal power. In Dublin there was barely a mention of George's anniversary. Trinity College, Dublin decided to fly the Union Jack alongside the Irish flag and its own standard and held a choral service on the day, but the decision was poorly received and extra police stood on duty as the tributes caused controversy.

India, too, would treat this Jubilee very differently. In 1897 its role at the heart of Victoria's empire had been integral to her Diamond celebrations. By 1935, Gandhi's salt march had begun the sustained popular demonstrations against British rule that would lead to independence the following decade. George emphasised the importance of India in his Jubilee broadcast but he was well aware by then of growing dissatisfaction with British rule in the country. However, he celebrated his Jubilee as a King and an Emperor.

Meanwhile, across Britain the number of people out of work continued to climb as economic depression marched on. In 1934 a new Unemployment Act had reversed a previous cut in dole while payment for benefits now came from national taxation rather than local rates. However, support was means tested with applications going before Public Assistance Committees whose unpopularity led to major demonstrations. As the Jubilee year began some economic commentators noted that George's anniversary coincided with twenty-five years of the Labour Exchanges which had been set up to help people find work. The King himself was only too aware that his Jubilee took place at a time of deep economic need which was changing his country just as deeply as war had.

This was reflected in the role that beneficence played in this celebration. The Jubilee of George III had been transformed by pressure from radical journalists to channel any money available for festivities into good causes as well as campaigns from social reformers to include the Biblical notion of forgiveness in the plans. George III's jubilee had seen collections to release debtors from prison and a pardon for prisoners of war. George V's celebrations saw local collections to support those in need but a nationwide appeal was also launched.

The King George Jubilee Trust Fund was set up to provide outdoor activities and gyms for teenagers across the country. It would support organisations already providing facilities and help them establish new branches. From its very beginning, however, it highlighted that traditional sources of charity in local areas were falling away. As it was launched, the Monarch's son and heir, the Prince of Wales, underlined in speeches that its works would take place in 'areas, rural as well as urban, where this kind of work has been held up from lack of public funds'.

In an interview to promote the Fund, the Prince touched on a sensibility being felt around Britain. Many found their finances strained and some local councils had heard complaints that the poor were being fed for the Jubilee at the expense of those not much better off themselves. Edward was explicit in the focus of the Fund, saying *'It is not an appeal for charity, but a tribute to the king from the countless people in this country who do not wish 1935 to pass by without leaving among us some living and permanent commemoration of this Jubilee year.'*

The organisers of the Jubilee were aware that asking those who felt in need themselves to help others might fall on deaf ears. Instead, this was billed a national tribute to a father figure with money going to work that might benefit everyone. Appeals for contributions for the Fund were still held at a local level with loyal mayors and councillors asking people to donate. But the main focus of the Jubilee Trust was at a national level and big fundraisers, like a 'Jubilee International' football match at Goodison Park between a side representing the Football League and another from Wales and Ireland, sprang up as Jubilee year went on.

Other problems were easier to deal with. A spate of parish and town councils ran into difficulties of an unexpected kind in the months leading up to the celebrations when caretakers, planning ahead, rummaged through the cupboards to find no Union Jacks available. In Northumberland, one official was so disgusted at the lack of town bunting that he sneeringly told a meeting that he might be able to lay his hands on 'half a Union jack' otherwise used to cover coffins. There was mild panic in Aldershot when the Town Clerk discovered, with days to spare, that there was no Union Jack to fly on Jubilee Day. The Mayor informed him that 'they must get one, somehow or somewhere'.

In Australia, the Governor of Victoria found his Jubilee levee snubbed by a large number of the Consular Corps who were still smarting from being placed in the last rank of precedence at a previous event. However, they all sent letters directly to the King to pay tribute to him on his anniversary and raised flags in honour of the Jubilee.

In fact, George received a wide range of international congratulations. Jubilees had been part of the Papacy and the Catholic Church for centuries and as George V marked his own, Pope Pius XI sent his congratulations, saying '*on this auspicious day, when*

*Your Majesty is celebrating with The Queen the Silver Jubilee of your reign over the peoples of the British Commonwealth, among whom you count millions of loyal Catholic subjects, we offer you our heartfelt felicitations for those twenty-five years of enlightened and beneficent rule, and we pray that God may bless you and the Queen with length of days and happiness and with consolation and success in your labours for the peace and prosperity of your realm.'*

President Roosevelt of the United States published his congratulatory message, telling George V that '*it is gratifying to contemplate the wise and steadfast influence which Your Majesty has exerted for a quarter of a century. The many traditions which we in the United States have in common with the British people permit us to understand how deeply stirring today's anniversary must be to Your Majesty's subjects, and we share in their rejoicing.*'

Even the President of France was gushing in his praise of the King. However, his message underlined another reason why George's Jubilee was getting notice on a global scale. Two decades earlier, he had been a wartime King. President LeBrun's message of congratulations on Jubilee Day included the exuberant words '*Your Majesty's name remains closely connected in the memories of all Frenchmen with remembrance of the gravest and most glorious hours which united the moral forces of our two countries. France is happy to associate herself with the striking homage rendered today by the British Empire to Your Majesty.*'

The Great War had informed another of the subtle changes apparent in this Jubilee. Communal feasting had been an integral part of the celebrations since the reign of George III but the big beef dinners of the nineteenth century were fading fast and not just because of protests like that of the London Vegetarian Society which wrote to a number of leading authorities asking them to cancel planned ox roasts. Simpler celebrations were in vogue as George's anniversary arrived and increasingly popular was something that would become a Jubilee staple – the street party.

In 1919 Britain had come together to mark Peace Day following the signing of the Treaty of Versailles. The focus of the celebrations had been children who had been left bereft by the war. Peace Parties were held with local communities coming together to put on a simple meal for them of tea, cakes and party food. As George's Jubilee plans reached their crescendo, that pattern was adopted for festivities for this royal anniversary.

In Luton the first events organised for the Jubilee, as 1935 got under way, were teas for all the school pupils in the area, while in Warwick priority was also given to parties for young people to mark George's anniversary. Communities across Norfolk, including those at Winterton, Long Stratton and Martham, all offered tea parties for children. In Portsmouth, a string of tea parties for children sprang up in streets across the city with the *Hampshire Telegraph* describing them as '*spontaneous affairs by local residents*'. These street parties were noted for their bright decorations as well as their food and drink, with the paper reporting 'some of the little streets had turned themselves into veritable tableaux for the occasion'.

And, just as there had been at the first British Royal Jubilee, there was an awareness that these celebratory events would provide a much needed meal for some of the poorest members of the community. In Tynemouth, just as plans for children's tea parties were being made to mark the Jubilee, it was reported that the number of pupils applying for milk and dinner at their schools was increasing sharply.

Despite protests from some, funding for local festivities was arranged on a local scale and followed that same Jubilee principle of making sure that the poor weren't out of pocket when celebrating their King. Around Britain, plans for fetes of all sizes took shape and the subtle creep of modernisation made itself felt. Alongside traditional games, like the sack races organised in Exmouth, there were new entertainments. In Portsmouth, games and sports were joined by a bus ride for some children as a treat while in Bradford, young people took part in a string of historic re-enactments to mark the occasion.

However, the focal point of the festivities was London. Newsreels of the time followed the transformation of the capital as over a mile and a half of scaffolding was erected on the route of the royal procession. An emphasis was placed on the work created for those in need of jobs by the celebrations. As the week of the celebrations began, buildings across the city revived that most important element of the first Georgian Jubilee, the illuminations. Over 150 buildings in central London alone took part and improvements in energy supply meant that this George's festivities were lit up far longer than those of his predecessor. Famous landmarks across the capital were illuminated throughout the Jubilee week with the streets around them closed to traffic every night from 9pm to allow spectators to enjoy the lights safe from the dangers of the ever encroaching motor car.

Buckingham Palace, St. James' Palace and the Tower of London all sparkled in the spring nights for the Jubilee as did Westminster Abbey, St. Paul's Cathedral and the newspaper industry's church of St. Bride's on Fleet Street. The well-heeled guests of the Savoy, the Dorchester and the Ritz were kept awake until midnight every night by the bright lights on the hotel fronts while the Monument, the Mansion House and the Royal Exchange also joined the celebrations. Australia House, South Africa House and Canada House were also lit up, underlining the role of Empire in this Jubilee. Further afield, Henry VIII's famous home at Hampton Court Palace also attracted large crowds of sightseers for its illuminations.

Competition for the best spots on the route of the royal procession was keen. The weekend before the Jubilee, newspapers published cut out and keep guides to the celebrations. The *London Daily News* dedicated a whole page to the route to be taken by the procession with a timetable, advising well-wishers of the most opportune moments to grab the best spot for a view of the royal party. The clock obsessed King's route was marked out on a map with specific timings while the paper repeated one message over and over again as the motor industry expanded. 'Be early, leave your car at home' it wrote on its front page.

As 6 May 1935 dawned, under clear skies and the promise of sunshine, tens of thousands were in place for the Jubilee procession, standing in flag decked streets to catch a glimpse of the King and Queen. The parade mixed tradition with change. The majority of the House of Windsor, along with visiting royalty, processed to St. Paul's by car and left from Clarence Gate. However, the upper echelons of George's dynasty made their way to the church service by carriage. The Duke and Duchess of York departed Buckingham Palace at 10.37am with the Prince of Wales, accompanying his aunt, the Queen of Norway, following at 10.42am precisely. They were well on their way by the time George V and Queen Mary set off, with the main carriage leaving at 10.54am on the dot. George's obsession with time was woven into his Jubilee party.

The first of the royal party arrived to huge cheers with particular attention on the Yorks and their two young daughters, Princess Elizabeth, who had just turned nine, and her little sister, Princess Margaret, who was a few months shy of her fifth birthday. There was also a big media interest in the newest member of the House of Windsor. Princess Marina of Greece had married the Duke of Kent seven months earlier. Known for her sense of fashion, her latest style pick was keenly anticipated although one newsreel commentator could only sum it up as a 'large, shady hat'.

The King and Queen travelled along Constitution Hill and through Piccadilly then along the north side of Trafalgar Square before heading to Duncannon Street, The Strand and Fleet Street which was decked with flags from across the Empire as well as bunting. There was also a stop on the boundary of the City of London where, as tradition demanded, the Lord Mayor presented the King with the pearl hilted Sword of the City which was duly returned before the procession went on.

King George V and Queen Mary approached St. Paul's to huge cheers. People had grabbed spots at windows and on balconies to join the celebrations. The famously unemotional Mary, decked in fur, seemed almost moved by the ovation.

The royal party entered St. Paul's beneath a canopy and between rows of Yeoman of the Guard. Royal trumpeters heralded their arrival before they made their way through the church and a congregation of over 4,000 people. Seated on throne-like chairs at the front of the congregation, with their granddaughter, Elizabeth, right behind them, George and Mary were suddenly bathed in bright shafts of sunlight as the service progressed, a moment captured in photographs sent around the world.

On their way back, having emerged to more cheers and the peal of bells, the royal party processed through Cannon Street, Queen Victoria Street and along the Embankment before heading to Northumberland Avenue and on to the Mall, allowing as many well-wishers as possible to see them. Almost as soon as the Palace gates closed on the carriage parade, thousands ran forward to get the best spot for the balcony appearance that followed. George and Mary were greeted by a wall of cheers as they made their way out to greet the people on their Jubilee. They were flanked by their children and grandchildren, a reminder of the dynasty George had fought to protect as well as a nod to the family image that helped the Windsors seem the same as the people whose support they needed to survive. George stood at its centre, the very image of 'Grandpa England', father figure to a new generation of royals as well as a nation.

In fact, George's Jubilee proved so popular and the King proved so keen to show his appreciation for the huge support he was given that he went on to make constant appearances on the balcony of Buckingham Palace in the days and weeks after his anniversary, striding out through the glass doors of the Centre Room almost on demand as May progressed.

George, with one eye on the future, was keen to see his family join his people at his Jubilee celebrations to underline the link between them. On the afternoon after his anniversary, the Prince of

Wales along with the Duke and Duchess of York attended a party for employees of Windsor Great Park. Princess Elizabeth and Princess Margaret grabbed the headlines as they sat with other children to watch a Punch and Judy Show while the Duchess of York, one of the most popular members of the Royal Family, was given a shrub by a 90-year-old who marked her birthday on Jubilee Day.

Another innovation followed as he began a series of small scale Jubilee visits. In the days after his celebrations, he and Queen Mary took Jubilee drives through different parts of London, again greeted by constantly large crowds. After arriving in another part of their capital by car, they would switch to a semi-state carriage and continue their procession to a meeting with local mayors. But George's popular touch was on show as he and his consort also insisted on being presented to the town clerks and other officials as well. One visit included his granddaughters, Princess Elizabeth and Princess Margaret, who were already darlings of the popular press.

Grand celebrations continued through the summer. A Jubilee Ball was held at Buckingham Palace in mid May while the Royal Family, including Elizabeth in a lace trimmed dress and holding her white gloves, mingled with guests at a garden party at the famous London residence. King George V and Queen Mary stood for hours to shake hands with as many of those invited as possible. Later in the summer, the King attended large military reviews as part of his Jubilee year, arriving on horseback for an army parade and despite the heat, and having turned seventy, bluntly refused a dismounting stool. Across the summer of 1935, he inspected army, navy and air force troops at special parades, marking his Jubilee as well as allowing him to honour the military which had served in the war and which had attended him on his anniversary.

But George had been showing his appreciation for the affection shown to him at his Jubilee since the day itself and as he instituted the greatest innovation of his celebrations, his broadcast, his deep gratitude almost caused him to lose his composure.

On the evening of 6 May 1935, the King spoke live to his country and his empire through the still relatively new medium of radio. Just a few words in, he stumbled and coughed but soon resumed his measured delivery of a heartfelt speech. The King was prone to colds but the brief wobble could well have been emotion. His address showed a man almost overcome by sentiment, a long way from the unfeeling character so often attributed to him.

Millions around the world listened as the King they had just feted spoke in humble tones of his gratitude for their well-wishes. There had been a run on radio sets in the weeks before as people prepared to join the Jubilee celebrations. No one was to be excluded. The Deaconess Hospital in Edinburgh allowed portable radio sets into each ward so that patients could join the celebrations. What they heard was a message striking for its simple language. George wanted his thanks to be understood in every home. His public image had been that of a kindly and supportive patriarch. As he gathered his Empire around him for this broadcast, he spoke to them without the pomp redolent of other royal addresses of the time. It would prove a masterstroke. His words, filled with emotion, would be widely praised. At just past 8pm on Jubilee Day, King George V said to his Empire:

> At the close of this memorable day, I must speak to my people everywhere. Yet, how can I express what is in my heart? As I passed this morning, through cheering multitudes, to and from St. Paul's Cathedral, as I thought there of all that these twenty-five years have brought to me and to my country and my empire, how could I fail to be most deeply moved? Words cannot express my thoughts and feelings. I can only say to you, my very dear people, that the Queen and I thank you from the depths of our hearts, for all the loyalty, and may I say, the love with which this day and always you have surrounded us.

I dedicate myself anew to your service for the years that may still be given to me.

I look back on the past with thankfulness to God. My people and I have come through great trials and difficulties together. They are not over. In the midst of this days' rejoicing, I grieve to think of the numbers of my people who are still without work. We owe to them, and not least to those who are suffering from any form of disablement, all the sympathy and help that we can give. I hope that during this Jubilee year, all who can, will do their utmost to find them work and bring them hope.

Other anxieties may be in store but I am persuaded that with God's help they may all be overcome if we meet them with confidence, courage and unity.

So I look forward to the future with faith and hope. It is to the young that the future belongs. I trust that through the Fund, inaugurated by my dear son, the Prince of Wales, to commemorate this year, many of them throughout this country may be helped in body, mind and character to become useful citizens.

To the children I would like to send a special message. Let me say this to each of them whom my word may reach. The King is speaking to you. I ask you to remember that in days to come, you will be the citizens of a great empire. As you grow up, always keep this thought before you and when the time comes, be ready and proud to give to your country, the service of your work, your mind and your heart.

I have been greatly touched by all the greetings which have come to me today from my Dominions and Colonies, from India and from this home country. My heart goes out to all who may be listening to me now, wherever you

> may be, here at home, in town or village, or in some far off corner of the Empire or it may be on the high seas.
>
> Let me end my words to you with those which Queen Victoria used after her Diamond Jubilee, thirty-eight years ago. No words could more truly or simply express my own deep feelings now.
>
> Form my heart, I thank my beloved people, may God bless them.

His decision to end his broadcast with the words of Queen Victoria underlined his determination to gently modernise the Jubilee while retaining all its classic elements and its impact cemented the success of this Jubilee and provided a lasting record of the celebrations.

In some ways, this anniversary broadcast summarised the secret of George's success, both in his Jubilee and his reign. He had deliberately cultivated a family image and taken a deep interest in the lives and politics of his Empire. His passion for the welfare of his citizens could be heard as his voice briefly faltered while talking of the impact of unemployment. Just days before speaking, he had given his approval to another scheme that would bring work to hundreds thanks to his Jubilee. The Jewish National Fund had raised £100,000 to pay for a forest to be planted in the Holy Land to mark the Jubilee. The announcement of the project confirmed that up to 1.5 million trees would be planted as a tribute and that some of the 500 who would be offered work on it would be German refugees. In a country still dealing with the aftermath of war, there was an echo of the Biblical remission of Jubilees in this gesture.

The speech had the desired effect. The following day, an editorial in *The Scotsman* wrote that *'yesterday gave the lie to the modern doctrine that the tradition of monarchy is effete. No matter how many Thrones about the world have crumbled to dust, the Throne which unites the British Empire is today solid and unassailable. It is a breakwater which the tides cannot shift and it will stand long after some of the systems of government which are being tried abroad are discarded or modified.'*

In Austria, which had lost its own imperial monarchy less than two decades earlier, the *Telegraf am Mittag* newspaper was also won over by George's Jubilee speech which it described as '*the most beautiful speech ever delivered by a king…a truly royal speech because it was so unroyal'*. In conclusion, the paper declared it *'the speech of a good man'*.

It became an important legacy of his Jubilee. The physical commemorations of his anniversary were limited, in part because of the economic climate and the determination to make this a moment of national celebration. George and Mary posed for official photos while Silver Jubilee walkways also became a popular tribute, but George's broadcast turned into a main plank of his celebrations. In fact, it made such an impression that, following George V's death just eight months later, it became the main selling point of a gramophone record of his speeches, released as a tribute to the King who had been so feted on that warm day in May.

But there was one more legacy of the Jubilee that would make its impact felt, well into the twenty-first century. During the ceremony at St. Paul's Cathedral, the King's eldest granddaughter, dressed in pink, sat behind him. Earlier, as she'd arrived with her parents, the British Movietone commentator noted the young princess 'lingers on the steps to take stock of the scene'. And as Queen Mary marshalled her family back into Buckingham Palace following the hugely popular appearance on the Jubilee afternoon, the same princess stayed put while others hurried in on Mary's orders.

Nine-year-old Princess Elizabeth clutched the edge of the balcony to take in the huge crowds that stretched down the Mall, cheering. Four decades later, she would be faced with another multitude, there to mark her own Silver Jubilee.

# Chapter Five

# The Silver Jubilee of Elizabeth II

Eight decades after Victoria had brought the Church of England to the steps of St. Paul's to save her ageing legs from a steep climb, Queen Elizabeth II strolled happily down its famous stairs to the cheers of a huge crowd. Dressed in bright pink, she left the Service of Thanksgiving for her Jubilee to a rapturous response and the prospect of another walkabout. She had already spent months touring her country and Commonwealth where she had shaken thousands of hands and listened to just as many voices. There was no rest in sight as Jubilee visits and tours continued throughout the year. The Silver celebrations of Elizabeth II were all about taking the Jubilee Queen to her people.

It was no surprise that this anniversary proved to be more energetic than any that had gone before it. The Queen was easily the youngest British Monarch to mark a Jubilee. George III had been seventy-one at the time of his Golden celebrations, Queen Victoria had marked her Jubilees at the ages of sixty-eight and seventy-eight while George V turned seventy soon after his Silver anniversary. In contrast, Elizabeth II was just fifty as the twenty-fifth anniversary of her reign arrived and turned fifty-one in her first Jubilee year. Her comparative youth gave organisers a new range of possibilities for celebrating the Jubilee Monarch.

Elizabeth also enjoyed far better health than the queen and kings who had marked these milestones before her. She had watched first hand as her own grandfather, George V, had struggled with ill health in the years before his own celebrations. Queen Victoria's Diamond Jubilee had been built around her increasing immobility but even at her Golden anniversary, she had appeared older than her age. The long years of seclusion following her widowhood had masked a growing infirmity, not helped by a growing girth. Meanwhile, the very first Jubilee Monarch, George III, was so poorly by the time his festivities began that he managed to take in only brief minutes of them before being confined to Windsor Castle once more. He had complained of not being able to see the spectacle laid on in his honour. His great, great, great, great granddaughter, Elizabeth II, would carry out her Jubilee according to the motto she had long held true to: *'I have to be seen to be believed.'*

The first four royal Jubilees had included festivities at a local level across Britain but the royal stars of the show had been confined to London and Windsor. The people had placed the Monarchy at the heart of homespun celebrations, but the majority hadn't come close to catching a glimpse of their Jubilee Queen or King. But as Elizabeth II marked her Silver anniversary in 1977, the decision was made to take the Jubilee to the people. It would turn into the biggest royal tour around the UK ever undertaken and run alongside visits across the Commonwealth which would transform Elizabeth II's anniversary into a global event.

The Queen had already travelled more widely than any British Monarch. Her twenty-five years on the throne had seen her undertake over thirty state visits, diplomatic events designed to boost relationships with other countries, as well as hosting another thirty or so in the UK. On top of that, she had made dozens of visits to Commonwealth countries by 1977, including five to Australia, four to New Zealand and ten to Canada. Her Silver Jubilee year would see her crisscross her realms for months, on visits totalling over 56,000 miles and witnessed by millions of well-wishers. It was a striking innovation.

Despite this change, the event retained much of the now established pattern. A Service of Thanksgiving, beacons and a balcony appearance were set as the jewels in the crown of a Jubilee day in London with street parties spreading the joy around the country. Loyal addresses, special stamps and coins and a formal portrait were all lined up. And before the Jubilee year even began, there was a striking reference to one of the original concepts of a jubilee, reconciliation, as well as a link by Elizabeth II to the King whose own anniversary had led to the creation of these royal celebrations, George III.

In the Queen's Christmas speech of 1976 she looked back on the trip she had made to the United States that year to mark the 200th anniversary of the Declaration of Independence. It had been an historic visit and Elizabeth II noted the links it provided between her and the first Jubilee king whose own celebrations had been a chance for his critics to re-focus on his loss of the American Colonies. The Queen put his actions at the heart of her first major speech on her Jubilee, saying on Christmas Day:

> Who would have thought 200 years ago that a descendant of George III could have taken part in these celebrations? Yet that same King was among the first to recognise that old scores must be settled and differences reconciled.

And the Biblical notion of a Jubilee being a time of remission and reconciliation came through in her words as she said:

> I would like my Silver Jubilee year also to become a special one for people who find themselves the victims of human conflict', *before adding* 'the gift I would most value next year is that reconciliation should be found wherever it is needed…if there is reconciliation, if we can get the climate right, the good effects will flow much more quickly than people believe possible.

Those good effects were needed. The United Kingdom was being called on to celebrate the anniversary of its Monarch but in one of its constituent nations, her very presence was anathema to one part of the population and the divisions over who should rule them had led to conflict. As 1977 approached, the Troubles in Northern Ireland were escalating and thousands had already died. Bombing campaigns had reached other parts of Britain while life for those in the province was led under the ongoing threat of attacks, often with little understanding from those outside. The political situation continued to intensify while relations between Britain and the Republic of Ireland were impacted by the conflict. The Queen had high praise for the work of the peace movement in Northern Ireland in her Christmas broadcast of 1976 but she could only hope for reconciliation as the Jubilee year unfolded.

There were other concerns, too. Like her grandfather, four decades earlier, the Queen was approaching the twenty-fifth anniversary of her reign at a time of economic hardship, rising unemployment and hikes in the cost of living. The pressures of paying for a nationwide party were being felt deeply.

It had been at the forefront of Labour Prime Minister Harold Wilson's first words on the celebration. When he confirmed the Jubilee would take place, in answer to a parliamentary question in December 1975, he noted that 'the Government have borne in mind Her Majesty's express wish that there should be no undue expenditure and that they trust it will also be taken into account by others who wish to organise celebratory events.'

But government was a big beast now. The Commons also heard that 'the cost of the central programme will be met by the appropriate departments and organisations from within existing expenditure limits'.

In an echo of Victoria's celebrations, where who paid for what was a major issue before the parties had even begun, the Prime Minister concluded 'it will not be possible for the Government to make additional or special contributions towards the cost of other events organised outside this central programme.'

This Jubilee was on a tight budget before it began.

But finances were just one part of the challenges around the Jubilee. There were calls, too, for debate on retaining the Monarchy. The first Jubilee had been driven by concerns that the bloody fall of France's royals might motivate a similar revolution in Britain. George V had seen a string of crowns tumble in his own reign and the violent death of several relations as a result, including the murder of his cousin and friend, Tsar Nicholas II of Russia. The Queen's own husband, Prince Philip, had seen his Greek Royal Family exiled just ten years before the Jubilee with their Crown abolished as the 1970s got under way. But no Jubilee Monarch had more experience of losing royal power than Elizabeth II. In her reign, a string of nations had chosen to reject her as Queen as she oversaw one of the most widespread moves away from colonial power in history.

In the previous ten years alone, she had ceased to be Queen of Ceylon, Queen of Sierra Leone, Queen of Gambia, Queen of Guyana and Queen of Malta when all those nations voted to become republics. The year before her Jubilee saw Trinidad and Tobago make the same decision. South Africa, Tanganyika, Uganda, Kenya, Ghana, Malawi and Nigeria had all removed her as their Monarch in the 1960s while her reign had been just a few years old when Pakistan cut its ties with the Crown and became a republic. There had been no objection and no criticism of any of these moves. Like her father, King George VI, before her, she had shown full support for nations making their own decisions, but the Queen who celebrated her Silver anniversary in 1977 ruled far less land than any of the previous Jubilee monarchs.

The past two Jubilees had taken Empire as a central theme. Elizabeth II's grandfather, King George V, had spoken to all his dominions on the night of his celebrations. The Diamond festivities of Queen Victoria had been turned into a quasi Festival of British Empire with all the Prime Ministers of her self governing dominions invited to London and made Privy Counsellors while the magnificent Jubilee parade which had brought the capital to a standstill had been made up, in large part, of colonial troops. Elizabeth II had seen her role in many nations change irrevocably in the years before her Jubilee. Even in the nations where she remained Queen, including Australia and Canada, there had been talk of cutting ties with the Monarchy. By 1977 Elizabeth II was a popular Queen but the institution she represented had its fair share of critics.

One the most high profile events of the Jubilee year would be the release of the single 'God Save The Queen' by the Sex Pistols. Its opening line became one of the most famous lyrics of the late twentieth century. 'God Save the Queen, and the fascist regime' blared out of homes and shops around the country, but it wasn't heard on too many stations as both the BBC and the regulator of Independent Local Radio banned it almost immediately. Claims abounded that hastily and temporarily altered rules on which record shop sales counted in the week when it was at its most popular had stopped it reaching number one on the official charts. However, it was perhaps even more noticeable as a number two record, with debate about whether it should have topped the charts keeping it a talking point. It cemented its place as the most high profile protest ever against a Jubilee.

It became, for some, the theme of the summer of 1977 which would see a Jubilee celebration like no other. In fact, the Silver festivities of Elizabeth II had already ripped up the rule book before they even got started. For the first time since Jubilees were introduced into British life in 1809, the main events didn't take place on the actual anniversary of the Monarch's succession.

Elizabeth II had become Queen on 6 February 1952 when her father, King George VI, died in his sleep at Sandringham. She preferred to keep the anniversary of his death privately. However, the problems of organising a Jubilee in the dark, cold days of February were immediately apparent and, very early on in the planning process, the decision was taken to hold the main part of her celebrations around the time of the Sovereign's official birthday in June.

It meant that the main focus of the celebrations would fall at a time already packed with prestigious pageantry that the world would want to see. Trooping the Colour and the Order of the Garter service both fell in June and would form part of a summer of ceremony. Just weeks before the long weekend, which would run from 4 June to 7 June 1977, the Queen was set to welcome NATO leaders to London as the city hosted the organisation's summit. It was also hoped the weather would be better for street parties and festivities. However, the natural break between the anniversary of the Queen's accession and the start of the major festivities provided a space for the long planned visits around the UK and Commonwealth that would come to define this celebration.

The Queen left the UK just four days after marking a quarter of a century of rule. The twenty-fifth anniversary of her accession, 6 February 1977, fell on a Sunday and she went to church where a larger than normal group of well-wishers awaited her. She was accompanied by Prince Philip, now the first male consort in British history to mark a Jubilee, and by the Prince of Wales, the Queen Mother and Princess Margaret. There was also a nod to the only other Queen, albeit consort rather than regnant, in British history to mark a Silver Jubilee – Elizabeth II's grandmother, Queen Mary. Pinned to the bright red coat chosen by the Queen for the day was the Cullinan V brooch with its heart-shaped diamond that she had inherited from Mary who had worn it on the day she was feted as Empress of India.

However, the dominions of the early twentieth century were now independent nations and part of a Commonwealth for which the Queen had always shown a particular devotion. On 10 February 1977 the first part of her Jubilee tours began, a six week stint that would take her half way around the world. Her stops in American Samoa and Western Samoa were followed by a visit to Tonga which had given up its status as a British protectorate just seven years earlier, the same year that her next destination, Fiji, had become independent. Elizabeth II was visiting as a fellow Head of State and as Head of the Commonwealth.

The Queen then arrived in New Zealand where the visit took on a more regal aspect. It also ran into protests including a demonstration in favour of a united Ireland. Against that backdrop, the major events of this Royal Jubilee visit continued. In Wellington the Queen of New Zealand held an investiture and opened Parliament, wearing a tiara created in 1973 with rubies given to her by the people of Burma.

She wore the same gems as she opened Parliament in Canberra eight days later at the start of a visit to Australia that would also take her to Sydney, Tasmania, Perth and New South Wales. A trip to Papua New Guinea, which in 1975 had become an independent state within the Commonwealth with Elizabeth II as its Sovereign, followed. The Queen was back in the UK for Easter but the respite was minimal. The Jubilee was now picking up pace.

In 1935, when Elizabeth was just nine and a spectator at her grandfather's Jubilee, tram companies had decked out some of their vehicles with illuminations as part of the celebrations. The 1977 interpretation saw London Transport paint twenty-five of its Routemaster buses silver for the Jubilee. They ran around the capital as a reminder of the celebrations, launched in April just ahead of the Queen's birthday.

Meanwhile, the Jubilee Monarch was juggling regular activities of State with celebrations. In April 1977 she hosted a State Visit from the King and Queen of Nepal and presented new colours to the First Battalion, The Scots Guards at Buckingham Palace. But as May started, so did the Jubilee celebrations proper.

On 4 May 1977, the Queen walked into Westminster Hall to receive the loyal addresses of the House of Commons and the House of Lords. Seated on a gilt throne, but with a peach and white hat rather than a Crown, she prepared to deliver one of the most important speeches of her Jubilee and its focus was on the alterations that had occurred in the years since her reign began.

> These 25 years have seen much change for Britain. By virtue of tolerance and understanding, the Empire has evolved into a Commonwealth of thirty-six independent nations, spanning five continents. No longer an imperial

> power, we have been coming to terms with what that means for ourselves and for our relations with the rest of the world.
>
> We have forged new links with other countries and in joining the European Economic Communities, we have taken what is perhaps one of the most significant decisions of my reign.

The speech also highlighted the ever changing aspect of her country, adding:

> The problems of progress, the complexities of modern administration, the feeling that Metropolitan Government is too remote from the lives of ordinary men and women, these among other things have helped to revive an awareness of historic national identities in these Islands. They provide the background for the continuing and keen discussion of proposals for devolution to Scotland and Wales within the United Kingdom.

But in the spirit of the first Jubilee and its themes of reconciliation, she ended by saying:

> A Jubilee is also a time to look forward! We should certainly do this with determination and I believe we can also do so with hope. We have so many advantages, the basic stability of our institutions, our traditions of public service and concern for others, our family life and, above all, the freedom which you and your predecessors in Parliament have, through the ages, so fearlessly upheld.

Some of those 'new links' were on show days later as she hosted the heads of NATO countries at a reception at Buckingham Palace, weaving Jubilee into the summit being held in London. The North Atlantic Treaty Organisation had come into being after the Second World War with member states agreeing to a policy of mutual defence in response to an attack on any member. At past Jubilees, Britain's military security had been bound up with that of the Empire. Now, it was partly dependent on an international alliance and the major member of that group was the United States, the country that had rejected the first Jubilee King, George III. Elizabeth II stood with US President, Jimmy Carter, at the evening gala although there was a minor controversy when he kissed the Queen Mother on the lips during the initial reception at the Palace.

There were more light hearted moments, too, with a parade of Rolls Royce cars at Windsor Castle and a series of visits to vintage aircraft shows. Meanwhile, the Canadian Mounted Police presented Elizabeth II with a horse, while the Chelsea Flower Show put on special Jubilee displays and showcased a brand new Silver Jubilee rose for its annual royal visitor.

The Queen stared back at her subjects from newspapers every day as a string of events made Jubilee headlines, while the launch of commemorative stamps and a growing number of souvenirs in the shops made the event feel omnipresent. Meanwhile, her heir was put at the forefront of a special campaign focused on another Jubilee tradition, charity towards others.

In an echo of her grandfather's Silver Jubilee, it was the Prince of Wales, rather than the Monarch, who led a charitable fund raising campaign to mark the anniversary. The Queen's Silver Jubilee appeal was launched by the Prince of Wales in April 1977. It aimed to raise funds to support young people and encourage them to serve their local communities. Prince Charles was given a plum slot on BBC One on a Sunday evening, speaking just before the latest in a series of 'Jubilee plays' marking the changes in society of the past quarter of a century – as well as the latest episode of hit sitcom, The Good Life. The launch of the appeal, which would lead to the creation of the

Queen's Silver Jubilee Trust (later The Queen's Trust), added another dimension to festivities that already had the air of one of the biggest events in post war Britain.

The Queen asked people to contribute to the fund rather than send her gifts and made it clear she wouldn't accept unofficial presents, although that didn't stop the flow of trinkets and tributes arriving at Buckingham Palace. Around the same time that she was receiving the loyal addresses of her Commons and Lords, royal officials were logging yet more unofficial gifts being sent to the Jubilee Monarch. One of the most popular items were coats for her corgis while Prince Philip was reported to have received more than one potion claiming to cure baldness. Each present was carefully recorded and then shared elsewhere.

More gifts were handed over, although this time face to face, as Elizabeth II and Prince Philip began their UK Jubilee tour. It would take them to thirty-six counties around the United Kingdom and become the most extensive royal visit to date. It began in Glasgow on 17 May 1977 with a Service of Thanksgiving at the Cathedral and a Civic Lunch at the City Chambers. However, the tradition of these ceremonies was accompanied by a range of more modern events, including a charity football match at Hampden Park.

Throughout the UK visits, ancient mixed with new. In Edinburgh, the Pageant of Scottish Youth welcomed the Queen but she also attended two banquets and, decked in a tiara, took a carriage ride through the city. On 27 May 1977 she received the loyal addresses of the Scottish Privileged Bodies before opening the new terminal building at Edinburgh Airport.

However, she also met some opposition. Scottish councils had been allowed to set their own Jubilee bank holidays and Aberdeen had chosen the Friday that the Queen would be in the area. Local shopkeepers were far from impressed with some saying they would stay open or risk losing their best day's trade in the week. However, others were more excited at the visit with George and Alice Wilson telling the *Aberdeen Evening Express* they hoped to meet the Queen on her visit to their old people's home so they could share the secrets of their seventy-four year marriage. Elsewhere in the city, a Jubilee concert was held alongside a series of special church services.

It was the first time that the Monarch had officially visited Scotland to mark a Jubilee. Elizabeth II returned to Windsor, the site of so many past festivities, for Silver anniversary celebrations as May came to an end. King George III had been feted with illuminations in this most royal of towns while Victoria sat in a carriage watching a statue of herself being unveiled. Among Elizabeth II's festivities were a trip to the circus at a special 'Big Top Show' for her anniversary. But interest in past celebrations was also taking hold. It had been four decades since Britain's last Jubilee and in London a special exhibition of memorabilia from all past royal anniversary festivities opened at Goldsmith's Hall.

The official anniversary programme also went on sale. It was produced by the King George Jubilee Trust, which had created all official souvenirs since 1935. Priced at 50p a copy, it promised that 35p from that would go to the Jubilee appeal launched by Prince Charles for his mother's celebrations. It contained a special message from the heir to the throne who, like the Queen in her Christmas speech, focused on the hope that the celebrations could bring reconciliation.

Meanwhile, newspapers and magazines began to publish their Jubilee specials. As the anniversary festivities began, the *Daily Mirror* offered its readers a '*giant Jubilee souvenir that you'll treasure forever*'. It was one of hundreds of special Jubilee inserts put into regular papers as a keepsake, another memento of a moment in time.

As at past Jubilees, souvenirs once again became big business. Tea towels, posters and mugs were among the most popular items while the usual spate of adverts appeared for bulk orders for Jubilee novelties, balloons and flags. Meanwhile, advertisers followed the well worn path of previous regal anniversaries by attaching the world Jubilee to anything they wanted to sell. A major change since the last celebrations of 1935 had been the invention of TV and plenty of producers created commercials for papers and magazines offering big deals on new sets bought in time to watch the Jubilee party.

The main celebrations came to life on 6 June 1977 as the Queen walked into Windsor Great Park to begin a Jubilee bonfire that would signal a string of beacons and fires being lit around the country. The interest in her Jubilee was evident as tens of thousands of people made their way, as the midsummer light began to fade, to stand in the park and try to catch a glimpse of the Monarch or her bonfire celebration.

Elizabeth II's grandfather, King George V, had begun his own celebratory chain of fire by pressing a button that triggered the electric lighting of a beacon. However, the Queen went back to basics, wielding a flaming torch to begin the bonfire for her Silver Jubilee. She also added an almost Victorian element to this part of her celebrations. Her great, great grandmother had insisted on the headwear she felt most comfortable in for her Jubilees and turned up to her festivities in a bonnet. For this anniversary special, the Queen wore a sensible coat and her favourite item of clothing, a headscarf.

However, the following day would see her in what would become one of the most emblematic outfits of her entire reign. Jubilee Day, 7 June 1977, saw the Queen dressed in pink by one of her favourite couturiers, Hardy Amies. Elizabeth II already employed the tactic of wearing something bright on big occasions so everyone present could see her but the choice of pink also mirrored the colour she had worn thirty-eight years earlier when she sat behind her grandfather, George V, in St. Paul's Cathedral for his own Silver Jubilee.

The dress and coat were complemented by a hat by Simone Mirman. The creation featured twenty-five bell shaped flowers at the back of a brim-free cap style design that allowed a full view of the face of the Jubilee Queen.

Elizabeth II seemed almost overcome as she began her anniversary procession down the Mall in the Gold State Coach. With the Duke of

A statue of George III had been commissioned for Weymouth at the turn of the 19th century but hidden away when he became ill. It was later turned into a Jubilee commemoration. *(By Colin Smith, CC BY-SA 2.0, https://commons.wikimedia.org/w/index.php?curid=98566481)*

George III, not long after his Jubilee. Although just 71 in 1809, years of ill health had left him frail and his failing eyesight meant he struggled to see any of the celebrations shown to him. *(Mezzotint by George Clint, after a painting by Thomas Stewardson – Public Domain, https://commons.wikimedia.org/w/index.php?curid=5824142)*

*Left*: A medieval imagining of Boniface VIII's proclamation of a year of remission in Rome, which came to be known as the Jubilee. *(Ignote, medieval miniature, Public domain, via Wikimedia Commons)*

*Below*: Jubilee illuminations took on a new aspect in 1935 when trams, like this one in Portsmouth, were lit up for the celebrations of George V. *(Mills & Co, Portsmouth, Public domain, via Wikimedia Commons)*

*Above*: George V and Queen Mary were joined by their four grandchildren for the balcony appearance on Jubilee day, among them Elizabeth who would mark her own Silver celebrations four decades later. *(J. Beagles and Co., Public domain, via Wikimedia Commons)*

*Below*: The K6 model of the phone box was a long lasting legacy of George V's Jubilee, designed in 1935 by Sir Giles Gilbert Scott to mark the Silver celebrations. *(By Victuallers - Own work, CC BY-SA 3.0, Wiki Commons)*

The Queen and the Duke of Edinburgh, seen on a walkabout in Hull in July 1977, continued their extensive UK visits for weeks after the actual Silver Jubilee weekend. *(By East Riding Archives, Wiki Commons)*

By 1977, the communal feasts of early Jubilees had been replaced by street parties, organised by neighbours. Tens of thousands of parties took place to mark the Silver celebrations of Elizabeth II. *(By Nicholas Mutton, CC BY-SA 2.0, Wiki Commons)*

*Above*: The Queen visited New Zealand in February 1977 as part of the first ever global tour to mark a British royal Jubilee. *(By Archives New Zealand from New Zealand - Queen Elizabeth II opening the Beehive, 1977, CC BY 2.0, Wiki Commons)*

*Below*: The traditional balcony appearance drew crowds of hundreds of thousands as Elizabeth II marked her Golden Jubilee in 2002. *(By Michael Pead, CC BY-SA 2.0 uk, Wiki Commons)*

The Queen Mother had been at Elizabeth II's side throughout the fifty years of her reign. Her death, along with that of Princess Margaret, at the start of the Golden Jubilee year led to an outpouring of sympathy for the Queen. *(By LSE Library, No restrictions, Wiki Commons)*

The Jubilee of 2002 was marked by some bus companies painting part of their fleet golden to bring the celebrations to the streets. *(By Basher Eyre, CC BY-SA 2.0, Wiki Commons)*

*Above*: The Diamond Jubilee medal of Elizabeth II, designed by Timothy Noad. *(By LA(Phot) Claire Myers – Defence Imagery, OGL v1.0, Wiki Commons)*

*Right*: Crowds gathered to watch a beacon being lit for the Diamond Jubilee at Robinswood Hill in Gloucestershire. Torches and fires have traditionally marked major royal events for centuries. *(By Mike Knapp, CC BY 2.0, Wiki Commons)*

The final balcony appearance of the Diamond Jubilee featured the 'slimmed down' Monarchy spoken of by Prince Charles but the compact family on show led to some criticisms. *(By Ben from London, England – Hello England, CC BY-SA 2.0, Wiki Commons)*

The Diamond Jubilee was one of the major events of 2012, with millions taking part in celebrations and catching up on other festivities while they rested. *(By Garry Knight, CC BY 2.0, Wiki Commons)*

Almost a century after Victoria's Golden Jubilee produced the first wave of mass souvenirs, commemorative gifts for the Silver celebrations of Elizabeth II had a familiar feel. *(By Maxwell Hamilton, CC BY 2.0, Wiki Commons)*

Advertisers became clever at incorporating Jubilees into all kinds of marketing as this commemorative medal from Victoria's Diamond Jubilee shows. *(Public Domain)*

The London Eye turned golden to mark the 50th anniversary of the reign of Elizabeth II, bringing the Jubilee tradition of illuminations to a modern landmark. *(By Christine Matthews, CC BY-SA 2.0, Wiki Commons)*

Victoria's daughter, Princess Louise, remained anonymous to enter a contest to design a Golden Jubilee statue of her mother for Kensington Palace. Her finished work showed a young queen, at the height of her power. *(Craig Michael Anstatt, CC BY-SA 4.0, via Wikimedia Commons)*

Victoria asked for two Indian servants to enter her household to mark her Golden Jubilee. One, Abdul Karim, became so influential that the queen's doctor tried to remove him just ahead of her Diamond Jubilee. *(Hills and Saunders, Public domain, via Wikimedia Commons)*

Victoria's Jubilee marked a half century of female power but some Jubilee celebrations ignored that and attempted to attribute her success elsewhere. *(Public domain)*

Although Victoria refused to wear a crown or tiara of any sort for her Jubilee appearances, some of the official photos she used showed her decked in diamonds.
*(W. & D. Downey (active 1855-1940), Public domain, via Wikimedia Commons)*

The only Jubilee Service of Thanksgiving to be held outside saw the area around St. Paul's Cathedral packed with the viewing seats in specially built stands among the most sought after in London. *(John Charlton, Public domain, via Wikimedia Commons)*

Victoria's Diamond Jubilee was the first to be caught extensively on camera. The Queen and her family had used photography to boost their image since its inception. *(London Stereoscopic & Photographic Company, Public domain, via Wikimedia Commons)*

*Above left*: The official Platinum Jubilee emblem was designed by 19-year-old Edward Roberts in regal purple and features St. Edward's crown. *(Edward Roberts)*

*Above right*: The Platinum Jubilee was the first time a 50p was used as a commemorative coin for the royal celebrations. *(The Royal Mint)*

As the Queen approached the 70th anniversary of her reign, she continued with high profile engagements including hosting G7 leaders during a summit in the summer of 2021. *(By UKinUSA from Washington, D.C, CC BY-SA 2.0, Wiki Commons)*

*Right*: King Karl XVI Gustaf and Queen Silvia of Sweden danced in the streets at the popular celebration for his Ruby Jubilee, which took place in Stockholm on 15 September 2013. *(Frankie Fouganthin, CC BY-SA 4.0, via Wikimedia Commons)*

*Below*: Queen Margrethe of Denmark's Ruby Jubilee, in 2012, included a carriage procession through flag-decked streets as well as a Service of Thanksgiving and a balcony appearance. *(Comrade Foot, CC BY-SA 2.0, via Wikimedia Commons)*

*Above*: The Queen on the day she became the longest reigning Monarch in British history – despite a lack of official celebrations, thousands still turned out to mark the moment with her in Scotland. *(By Scottish Government, CC BY 2.0, Wiki Commons)*

*Below*: Jubilees were a chance to 'be seen to be believed' but the rise of social media has made royalty more visible than ever, as was seen when the Obamas visited Kensington Palace in 2016. *(By The White House from Washington, DC – P042216PS-0680, Public Domain, Wiki Commons)*

Edinburgh at her side, she progressed through London to cheering crowds as eight grey horses drew the carriage, first commissioned two centuries earlier by George III. Just behind the gilded coach rode the heir to the throne, the Prince of Wales, in the uniform of the Welsh Guards.

This regal procession was surrounded by Beefeaters and Yeoman of the Guard while massed ranks of the Armed Forces followed behind. Just as George V and Victoria had done, the Queen stopped at the boundaries of the City of London to be presented with the ceremonial sword before continuing on her way to St. Paul's for the national Service of Thanksgiving for her reign. And all the way, hundreds of thousands of people cheered and clapped in streets decked with flags and bunting.

Waiting for the Queen at St. Paul's Cathedral were her Royal Family. They had led the procession with Princess Anne and Captain Mark Phillips in the first carriage, followed by Princess Margaret. The Queen Mother, dressed in bright yellow, had ridden with Prince Andrew and Prince Edward. Accompanying them were the Household Cavalry and a division of the Canadian Mounted Police.

The congregation of 2,700 included leading politicians, Prime Minister James Callaghan, as well as Commonwealth leaders and foreign ambassadors and other Heads of State, among them President Jimmy Carter, this time better briefed on protocol. They sang 'All People that on Earth do dwell' as the Queen and her consort processed down the aisle. The service, led by the Bishop of London, saw Elizabeth II kneel for a blessing, another sharp contrast to her predecessor, Victoria, who had been unable to step from her own carriage at the same church all those years before.

Just seven years earlier, the Queen had instigated a new royal tradition, the walkabout. The first had taken place during a tour of Australia in 1970 but had quickly become a fixed point of royal visits. The Silver Jubilee day of Elizabeth II would see her carry out an elongated meet and greet with some of the thousands crammed into the City of London to see her. She made her way to the Guildhall for a lunch, hosted by the Lord Mayor, in which she gave a moving speech:

> When I was twenty one, I pledged my life to the service of our people and I asked for God's help to make good that vow. Although that vow was made in my salad days, when I was green in judgement, I do not regret nor retract one word of it.

It was an acknowledgement of her changing role as Monarch. Not only had much altered during her reign but this twenty-fifth anniversary also signalled a new phase in her rule. Elizabeth II, the young Queen thrust on to the throne by the untimely death of her father, was now an experienced Head of State and moving into the second quarter century of her reign with a fresh confidence borne of experience but always with the same sense of service.

Another hugely popular procession back to Buckingham Palace ended with an appearance on the balcony with Elizabeth II surrounded by her whole family again. But as they prepared to make their farewells, one person lingered at the side of the Jubilee monarch – the Queen Mother watched with pride as her elder daughter was feted by millions.

Meanwhile, around the country, street parties took place to mark the Silver anniversary of Elizabeth II. The heart of Jubilee celebrations had always been the popular festivities that sprang up to mark these monarchical milestones and the twenty-fifth anniversary of Elizabeth II turned that into an artform. The street party came into its own with 4,000 taking place in London alone on that Jubilee day.

They took on a very different hue to the communal celebrations of the earliest Jubilees. While ox roasts and village teas remained, they were smaller in number. Instead, the vogue for the very local celebrations held sway. Streets came together to put on parties with furniture taken out of front rooms and kitchens to provide an impromptu celebration and households contributing feasts of party food. Fancy dress contests and discos had replaced the village sports contests of past Jubilees.

Also gone was the notion of the rich feeding those less well off to mark the royal anniversary. Most street parties were self generated and self funded. In Lynn in Norfolk, preparations had begun early with organisers collecting 10p per child per week in the run up to the street celebrations, while Jubilee Street in Newbury, Berkshire felt the pressure to live up to its name and held a children's party with two celebration cakes as well as a commemorative crown for all attendees.

However, it wasn't all plain sailing. Jubilee Road in Reading was criticised for putting up 'two solitary Union Jacks'. The *Diss Express* wrote a sharp editorial just days before the Jubilee, attacking those who weren't happy at private celebrations being set up for the anniversary. Describing the complaints as 'petty wrangling', it noted that the Coronation had been celebrated by small communities in the area and this Jubilee should be no different. Celebration by committee was starting to fade into history.

So, too, were commemorative statues. While Victoria's Jubilees had been celebrated with a spate of likenesses, there had been a notable dropping away of similar memorials at the time of the first Silver Jubilee, that of George V in 1935. That pattern continued as Britain marked its second twenty-fifth monarchical anniversary. Instead, the permanent mementoes took on a more modern aspect. A new Tube line, planned long before the celebrations, would end up being named Jubilee in honour of the Queen's anniversary although the official opening, by the Prince of Wales, didn't take place until 1979. Land on the south bank of the Thames which had housed the Dome of Discovery during the last great set piece event of King George VI's reign, the Festival of Britain, was transformed into a Jubilee Garden. Meanwhile, some of the most iconic landmarks in London were at the heart of a new walkway, designed to mark the Jubilee.

On 9 June 1977, Elizabeth II and Prince Philip sailed down the Thames in a river progress organised by the Port of London Authority. The Queen's vessel, the *Nore*, was dressed as a royal barge and stopped several times for her to meet mayors of local London boroughs. It had echoes of the first Queen Elizabeth and reached its full regal splendour as the second Elizabeth passed the Tower of London to the sounds of a 62-gun salute. The Jubilee Queen hosted a lunch on board HMS *Britannia* and opened the Silver Jubilee walkway that would become a permanent memento of her celebrations. She returned to the river that evening to review a river pageant featuring over 140 boats.

However, just days earlier, the Thames at been at the heart of another demonstration against the Jubilee. The Sex Pistols had sailed down the river as Elizabeth II walked through the city at the height of her Silver festivities. Police boats brought them to the river bank and several arrests were made. But the mood of the country was firmly set on celebration. As June continued, the Queen carried out a string of Jubilee engagements with Lancaster and Liverpool among the eight places visited in just two days. She spent three days in Wales before overseeing royal reviews of the Royal Navy and the Royal Cadet Forces.

The following month included a review of the Royal Air Force as well as Jubilee visits to over thirty more towns and cities around the UK. The celebrations continued when the Queen, on a rare visit to the tennis championships at Wimbledon, found herself in the Royal Box on Centre Court on the day that Virginia Wade won the Ladies' Singles. Elizabeth II, whose own father had played at the championships long before taking the throne, presented the silver Venus Rosewater dish to her in what would become one of the most celebrated images of her Jubilee year.

The Jubilee tours which had been such an innovation for this celebration continued through August as the Queen and the Duke of Edinburgh visited the South West of England with a royal review of the Royal Marines also taking place.

They spent several days in Northern Ireland where a garden party in Coleraine saw the Queen introduced to several people who had lost loved ones in the Troubles. The Queen returned to her wish for reconciliation in a speech at the University of Ulster when she said:

> Those with different beliefs and aspirations understand that if this community is to survive and prosper they must live together and work together in friendship and forgiveness.

The final Jubilee visits took the Queen to the Commonwealth once more. She opened the Canadian Parliament in October during a five day visit to the country before heading off for a two week tour of the Caribbean that would include stops in the Bahamas, the British Virgin Islands, Barbados, Mustique and Antigua and Barbuda. She returned to the UK just in time for another major milestone in this Jubilee year.

Just weeks before Jubilee weekend, the Queen's only daughter, Princess Anne, announced she was expecting her first child. The baby would be fifth in line to the throne and a first grandchild for the Queen and the Duke of Edinburgh and despite confirmation that the baby would have no title, their arrival would guarantee the direct line of succession to the throne of Elizabeth II.

That guarantee came on 15 November 1977 when Princess Anne gave birth to a son. Peter Mark Andrew Phillips was welcomed to the world with a 41-gun salute at the Tower of London and made his debut several days later as he left hospital with his mother. He bawled his way through a photo call soon after his christening at Buckingham Palace on 22 December 1977 with the Queen first among those trying to sooth him.

Days later, she would speak once more to her country and Commonwealth in a Christmas broadcast that brought down the curtain on her Jubilee year. She thanked all those who had celebrated with her but underlined her belief that the festivities had succeeded because they were for everyone, as she remarked:

> The street parties and village fetes, the presents, the flowers from the children, the mile upon mile of decorated streets and houses; these things suggest that the real value and pleasure of the celebration was that we all shared in it together.

She returned once more to that Jubilee theme, reconciliation, with special mention of her time in Northern Ireland and renewed wishes for a coming together of communities. Her final words reflected on peace as she made reference to the beacons that had begun her festivities and said *'my hope this Christmas is that the Christian spirit of reconciliation may burn as strongly in our hearts during the coming year'*.

The celebrations for the Silver Queen were over but they had made a mark that would become a staging post in her reign and in the life of the country that witnessed them with her. The energy of a new celebration had reinvigorated the now established practice of Jubilees for another generation.

# Chapter Six

# The Golden Jubilee of Elizabeth II

On a summer's evening, the soaring notes of an electric guitar ripped through the clear, still air. 'God Save The Queen' filled the skies above London while thousands of voices below joined in. A massive concert marking Elizabeth II's Golden Jubilee was under way. Brian May stood on top of that most royal of buildings, Buckingham Palace, playing the national anthem with a global audience of millions looking on. The sight of the Queen guitarist paying tribute to the Queen became an iconic image that seemed to sum up the gratitude that had come to mark the celebrations for fifty years of the new Elizabethan age. And yet just months before, this same Jubilee had been written off as a disaster waiting to happen.

The pessimism had seemed well placed. The Monarchy of Elizabeth II was still recovering from a blow that had left people around the world questioning whether it could survive. The death of the Queen's former daughter-in-law, Diana, Princess of Wales, in August 1997 had seen the grief that marked her passing turn to anger against an institution that was accused in some quarters of casting her out and leaving her vulnerable. Sympathy rested with her sons, still teenagers, while the older generation were painted as uncaring and out of touch. The Queen had worked hard to rally against that but less than five years after the death of Diana stunned the world, the Royal Family was still rebuilding.

But Diana wasn't the only factor in the questions over whether Britain, never mind the Commonwealth, was ready to celebrate a Jubilee. The UK was still 'Cool Britannia' and the new focus on national identity meant the Union Jack was more likely to be seen on a pop star's dress than flying in a back garden. The pomp, ceremony and circumstance created around the Monarchy were all in vogue but not because of the royals. Meanwhile, in some of Elizabeth II's other realms, including Australia and New Zealand, celebrating a culture rooted in the past was very far from fashionable. Ongoing debates about shaking off the rule of a woman who was based tens of thousands of miles away had continued to grow as the Jubilee approached.

Like all institutions, the Monarchy had seen its fortunes dip in other ways. The Royal Family was led by a 76-year-old woman, supported by her 82-year-old husband and 101-year-old mother. Even her heir was middle aged, celebrating his fifty-third birthday just months before the Jubilee was set to take place. The Prince of Wales was also trying to introduce his long-term partner, Camilla Parker Bowles, to public life against a backdrop of commentary over whether the two should be allowed to marry. Meanwhile, his youngest brother, Prince Edward, and his new wife, had attracted criticism of their own as the Countess of Wessex was caught in a newspaper sting, promising access to the Queen.

Surrounded by so many ongoing controversies, the Royal Family's prospects of selling a sparkling celebration of a half century of rule looked slim as 2001 came to an end and the Jubilee year itself approached. When the person chosen to co-ordinate the celebrations, Lord Levene of Portsoken, quit his post amid claims he was unhappy with the way plans were proceeding, the situation looked ominous. Tony Blair's government denied the project was in chaos but opposition politicians made capital of it.

The Queen kept calm and carried on. Her Christmas Speech of 2001 gave a gentle indication that the party would go ahead, whatever difficulties surrounded it. *'I hope that in the months to come we shall be able to find ways of strengthening our own communities as a sure support and comfort to us all – whatever may lie ahead.'* Her words would turn out to be almost prophetic.

This would be the most ambitious Golden Jubilee Britain had ever seen. While the celebrations of King George III had been innovative, they were a relatively small-scale event. The country's only other Golden Jubilee, that of Queen Victoria in 1887, had been spread across several days, but even that had come nowhere near the plans for Elizabeth II's half century of rule which would stretch on for months and see the Monarch travel over 40,000 miles around the world. As 2002 began, it seemed the scale of the proposed party could be its undoing before it even began.

As the government confirmed its proposals for the celebrations, on 8 February 2002, it put an emphasis on a sense of community and a 'people's Jubilee'. The Queen and the Duke of Edinburgh would travel around the UK and the Commonwealth throughout the year, meeting as many people as possible and visiting a wide range of groups and places. At the heart of the celebrations would be a four-day extravaganza centred on London which would include several major events where the doors of Buckingham Palace would be thrown open for thousands to celebrate alongside Elizabeth II, as well as a carnival style parade which would involve thousands more. The Prime Minister also announced how Lottery funding would be made available to groups and communities to help them plan and put on Jubilee celebrations. And there was a Jubilee first – in a sign of the times, the whole event was given its own website.

Within twenty-four hours, the party mood was gone. On 9 February 2002, Buckingham Palace announced that the Queen's only sister, Princess Margaret, had died at the age of seventy-one. The Royal Family went into mourning although no state observances were made. The funeral of the princess, who had been ill for some time, took place on 15 February 2002 at St. George's Chapel. The press focused on the Queen Mother who had rarely been seen in recent times and who was photographed being flown in by helicopter for the funeral of her younger child. Having said her final farewells and comforted her mother, the Queen left Windsor to begin the celebrations for her Golden Jubilee with a string of visits to Commonwealth countries.

Three countries and three very different receptions followed. Elizabeth II arrived in Jamaica on 18 February 2002 with the Duke of Edinburgh at her side. The country had become independent forty years earlier, declaring her as its Queen at the same time and remaining a member of the Commonwealth. The Queen would describe the visit, which ended with a power cut during a banquet, as memorable. Alongside supportive crowds, she faced protesters who wanted an end to the Monarchy as well as reparations for the slave trade.

The Queen's focus throughout her four days on the island was unity. In an historic address to the Jamaican parliament on 19 February 2002, she reflected on the very fact that her Jubilee was being marked.

> Such anniversaries are important, they are, I hope, opportunities to celebrate and, in so doing, to bring people and communities together. They are also moments to reflect on what has gone before and to rededicate ourselves with determination and confidence to all that lies ahead.

However, confidence in her rule was less certain on her next stop. As she touched down in New Zealand for a five-day visit, the country's Prime Minister was absent. Helen Clark had left for a series of meetings in Europe and just hours before the Queen flew into Wellington, she told a gathering at the London School of Economics that 'The idea of a nation such as New Zealand being ruled by a head of state some 20,000km away is absurd. It is inevitable that New Zealand will become a republic. It is just a matter of when the New Zealand people are bothered enough to talk about it – it could be ten years, or it could be twenty years, but it will happen.'

Crowds were notably smaller for much of the New Zealand visit and the Queen seemed to touch on the changing nature of the country's relationship with the Royal Family as she addressed a state dinner in Wellington.

> This is a very different country from the one I first visited all those years ago. The changes here over these fifty years have been dramatic; I have admired your increasing energy and confidence. I know that this process of evolution will continue as you, the people of New Zealand, map out your path for the future in your own time and in your own way.

Even if the years to come seemed uncertain, a level of respect for the service of the Queen over half a century remained. Helen Clark returned in time to meet the Sovereign before she left for Australia on 27 February, but her arrival in Adelaide brought more troubles. She was greeted by Peter Hollingworth, Governor General of Australia, who was under intense pressure over allegations he had failed to investigate claims of child sex abuse in the Anglican Church when he had served as Archbishop of Brisbane. Protesters against his ongoing role shouted their disapproval of him and his ultimate boss, Elizabeth II, as she began her five-day visit.

Australia had recently seen an upsurge in republican sentiment and the Queen reflected on that as she addressed a reception at Adelaide Festival Hall.

> Whatever may lie ahead, I declare again here tonight that my admiration, affection and regard for the people of Australia will remain, as it has been over these past fifty years, constant, sure and true.

Against that continued acknowledgement that feelings towards the Monarchy could continue to change as her reign went on, the Queen officially opened the Commonwealth Heads of Government

Meeting which took place in Coolum in Queensland. However, even her devotion to the Commonwealth came under strain as her Golden Jubilee year began. The event had originally been scheduled for October 2001 but was postponed following the 9/11 attacks. Elizabeth II flew into a major security operation while one of the main focuses of the meeting would be the erosion of democracy in Zimbabwe.

The deep and sometimes difficult nature of her role and reign seemed to be played out across the media in her main Commonwealth tour for this Jubilee. The complex politics with which she was often involved as an observer and adviser almost eroded the ceremonial that was integral to her public image. Coverage in UK papers was largely positive but a nagging sense that the celebrations would struggle to inspire the public shows of support expected at big events like a Jubilee continued to grow. The unveiling of a new portrait of the Queen as Head of the Commonwealth, soon after her arrival back in London in early March 2002, attracted far less attention than the ongoing rows about the future of the Crown in countries like Australia and New Zealand.

The Queen had more personal concerns to occupy her. The health of her mother was continuing to cause concern as she struggled to shake off a cold that had bothered her for months. She retired to her home at Royal Lodge in Windsor where she died in her sleep on the afternoon of 30 March 2002 with her remaining daughter at her side. The Queen Mother's coffin was taken to Westminster Hall to lie in state and it was during these darkest days that Elizabeth II's fortunes began to turn.

The loss of the wartime queen who had won the hearts of thousands with her visits to the bombsites of the East End proved a pivotal moment in the popularity of the Royal Family. Tributes began to pour in while long queues formed to walk past her coffin. By the time her four grandsons took their positions at each corner of her catafalque in a moving tribute on the eve of her funeral, over 200,000 people had paid their last respects to the matriarch of the House of Windsor.

When the Queen led her family out for the final farewell, on 9 April 2002, a wave of sympathy for the grief-stricken Monarch had taken hold. Crowds lined the streets of London to say goodbye and amidst the pomp and ceremony was a wreath of white flowers with a card signed 'Lilibet'. The use of her childhood name in this most regal of circumstances struck a chord with many. In the depths of her grief, the wave of affection directed at the Queen hinted at a regard for her which would change the nature of the Jubilee.

However, the signs that this celebration of her reign might not be the wash-out being talked about in the early part of 2002 were already there, if somewhat hidden from view. The day after the Queen Mother's death, 31 March 2002, had long been set as the deadline for street party applications. The gloomy reports in the first weeks of the year of low numbers and a lack of interest had obscured a reality that would see thousands of communities across the UK apply to hold these very British celebrations. Worcester City Council became the first to waive all fees associated with holding Golden Jubilee street parties and local authorities around the country began to follow suit. Eventually, forty thousand toolkits for community events were distributed and local websites began to carry ever increasing listings of planned street closures for parties in the making.

Applications for tickets to the main events on the Jubilee weekend were also flooding in. There were 12,500 places available at the classical Prom at the Palace, set for 1 June, but organisers found themselves with over two million requests. The Party at the Palace, scheduled to take place two days later, was just as well subscribed. Applications for both events would end up breaking records.

The Jubilee began to seep into everyday life with mementoes from biscuits to beer finding their way into the shops. The official souvenir programme was published on 24 April and a special £5 commemorative coin was produced. A series of official pictures began to appear with eleven photographers, including Canadian singer Bryan Adams and

Australian artist Polly Borland, commissioned to capture a likeness of Elizabeth II for posterity.

The gentle creep of the Jubilee was in some ways reminiscent of the build-up to Queen Victoria's golden celebrations over a century earlier. While major events had been planned to mark both anniversaries, the countdown to those box office days involved a seemingly incessant spread of little things that anyone and everyone could take part in. At the heart of both historic times was a realisation that without popular participation, the party would fall flat. Whether it was buying a sweet tin with an already familiar photo of the Monarch on its front or tucking away commemorative stamps for future generations, small actions, accessible to all, helped to knit both Jubilees into the public consciousness before the pomp and ceremony even began.

By the time Elizabeth II officially started her Jubilee celebrations, the tide had turned in her favour. The set piece events got under way just a month after the death of her mother but the Queen was ready for the show.

On the evening of 29 April, decked in diamonds, she attended a dinner with all her living Prime Ministers, past and present, at Downing Street. It was a mere warm up act for the first proper ceremonial of the Golden Jubilee. Just hours later, she entered the Palace of Westminster for an historic address to both Houses of Parliament.

Elizabeth II sat on a gilded throne on the ancient steps of Westminster Hall, her loyal consort at her side and the pageantry of a thousand years as her backdrop. Trumpeters in golden uniforms heralded her arrival while the Yeoman of the Guard, in their crimson and gilt coats, kept guard over the Monarch. Just below her and in full traditional dress were the Lord Chancellor and the Speaker of the House of Commons. MPs and peers sat in neat rows before her, spread out across the famous stone floor where her predecessors had sometimes battled for the right to retain their Crown. The history of the most famous Monarchy in the world had been brought together for a showstopping start to the Golden Jubilee.

It was also the setting for one of the most important speeches of the Queen's year. It was only the fifth time that she had addressed parliament of her own accord and her focus was on the ever-evolving nature of the country she had now ruled for half a century. The Queen spoke of her gratitude to those who helped her, adding:

> For if a jubilee becomes a moment to define an age, then for me we must speak of change – its breadth and accelerating pace over these years.... change has become a constant; managing it has become an expanding discipline. The way we embrace it defines our future.

No one was more aware of the impact that the Jubilee could have on the future of the Monarchy than Elizabeth II. May began with the first of dozens of visits across the UK that she and the Duke of Edinburgh undertook through the summer of 2002. As in 1977 and the Silver Jubilee tours, their aim was to meet as many people as possible as their time as Monarch and consort was celebrated. But in 2002, the mood had shifted. Buckingham Palace was keen to emphasise the diversity of their trips and of those they encountered.

This was to be more than the flag waving, bunting decked visits of her first major anniversary which had taken its cues from the Jubilee of her grandfather, George V. That change which had featured so heavily in the Queen's speech to parliament was to inform her latest UK wide tour. There were addresses to the new Scottish and Welsh parliaments as well as a speech to MLAs in Belfast. Alongside museum openings and art events, there were religious celebrations including a visit to a mosque as well as a Hindu and a Sikh temple and an interfaith reception at Buckingham Palace. The Queen spent time on allotments in east London set up to support people with learning disabilities and on the set of soap opera, Emmerdale, as she crisscrossed the country.

Elizabeth II was the oldest Monarch to celebrate a Golden Jubilee, turning seventy-six just as the major commemorations got under way. However, her diary was packed out. In the first week of her UK tours, she visited Cornwall, Devon, Somerset, Buckinghamshire, Berkshire, Durham and Tyne and Wear and would go on to tour fifty counties and seventy cities between May and August 2002. The royal train racked up 3,500 miles carrying the Queen to her anniversary visits while she and Prince Philip took on fifty-five walkabouts during the Jubilee trips.

If the start of the year had seen media in the UK dominated by questions over the success of the anniversary to come, as spring gave way to summer, print and broadcast outlets were all awash with sunny stories of a seemingly ever-present Queen. As well as the Jubilee visits, Elizabeth II continued with the traditional pattern of royal life leading to weeks where not a single day passed without a high-profile event focused on her. As May took hold, she headed to the Royal Windsor Horse Show for two days of events. Within hours of that event ending, she was at the Chelsea Flower Show. Less than twenty-four hours later, the Queen opened a new gallery at Buckingham Palace while the day after that saw her at the Royal Academy of Arts. She then arrived in Scotland, where she would attend engagements in the Borders and the Western Isles as well as Edinburgh, Glasgow and Dundee. There was a garden party at Holyroodhouse as well as services of thanksgiving for her reign. And in between it all, she opened the Jubilee Wheel, just one monument which was named in honour of the Queen and her anniversary as the year went on.

Among the other permanent marks left as the celebrations took hold were streets across the UK renamed as Elizabeth, Jubilee, Golden or Royal. Hospitals, hotels and parks were given new names while five towns around the UK started changing their signage having been given city status to mark the fiftieth anniversary of the Queen's reign. A new focus on celebrating this royal anniversary in as many places outside London had been a hallmark in early planning but by

June, and the main Golden Jubilee weekend, all eyes were on the capital once more.

Queen Victoria had innovated by using the balcony at Buckingham Palace for public appearances. Her own Golden Jubilee, one hundred and fifteen years earlier, had seen her lead her family out to wave to cheering crowds. Now, her great, great, great, great granddaughter would continue that tradition. For the first time, the gardens of Buckingham Palace were opened to the public for a major concert. On the evening of 1 June 2002, the first of the four-day extravaganza marking fifty years of Elizabeth II's reign, the lawns were covered in picnicking partygoers as the Prom at the Palace began.

The Queen and the Duke of Edinburgh swapped a picnic blanket for an improvised royal box where they were joined by the Royal Family. If the appetite among politicians for a Jubilee jolly had been limited as 2002 got under way, the desire to be part of this royal milestone had appealed to stars from across the Commonwealth with New Zealand opera singer Kiri Te Kanawa leading the cast. A UK TV audience of over five million tuned in that Saturday night. The Jubilee party was underway.

Among the performances they heard was a rendition of Handel's Zadok the Priest, the same music which had echoed through Westminster Abbey as Elizabeth II was crowned. On 2 June 2002, exactly forty-nine years after her Coronation, the Queen was at another ancient church with royal links as she gave thanks for her reign at a special service at St. George's Chapel, Windsor alongside the Duke of Edinburgh. Again, with an eye on inclusion, members of the Royal Family travelled to other parts of the UK to join in thanksgivings for the Jubilee. The Prince of Wales headed to Swansea where he was joined by his two sons, Prince William, 19, and Prince Harry, 16, at St. Mary's Church, while the Princess Royal travelled to Ayr in Scotland. The Earl and Countess of Wessex attended a similar ceremony in Salisbury. Meanwhile, across the UK and

Commonwealth, special prayers were said for a Monarch who had never made any secret of her own personal religion.

In the run up to the celebrations, Buckingham Palace had emphasised the importance that would be placed on faith and belief during the anniversary year. It was a reflection not just of Elizabeth II's own viewpoint but an important part of constructing a Jubilee. With its origins in the Bible, the very notion of marking a significant milestone in a royal reign had been founded in religious thanksgiving. The Queen, as a young Princess, had walked into Westminster Abbey to take part in a special service marking her own grandfather's Silver Jubilee. Although this day of reflection would turn out to be the quietest of the main Golden Jubilee weekend, it was among the most significant for the Queen herself.

Britain woke to the first of two Bank Holidays on 3 June and thousands of communities prepared to start their street parties which, in some cases, would go on for several days. The Queen began her day at Windsor Castle before visits to Eton and Slough. She was back in London by the afternoon, helping start a national singalong with tens of thousands joining a countrywide version of 'All You Need is Love' by the Beatles. Her already historic reign had seen music change dramatically through its long course and many of the acts which had made British pop world famous would take part in the Party at the Palace that evening.

Brian May's rendition of 'God Save the Queen' was the opening salvo in a night that would see Cliff Richard, Tony Bennett and Paul McCartney take to the stage. Another 12,000 ticket holders, picked from a ballot, took their seats for the event, with hampers including the newly created 'Jubilee chicken' handed out to keep them going through the long evening. Another full Windsor house settled into the royal box and in the background could be seen a face that signalled the royals were preparing to move on, for also on the guest list was Camilla Parker Bowles. Although she sat separately from the Prince of Wales, several rows back next to Princess Alexandra and her husband, her appearance was taken as another sign of growing acceptance within the House of Windsor of the long-term status of her relationship with the heir to the throne. The decision of the Queen to include her son's partner underlined, again, her awareness of this Jubilee as a transitional moment for the Monarchy. Amidst the celebrations, she continued to put a focus on reshaping royalty for the challenges of the new century which had just dawned.

The last act of this hectic Jubilee day was to reshape another royal tradition. For centuries, beacons had been lit to mark major events, from the births of longed – for heirs to the news of vital military victories. The first modern British Jubilees, those of Queen Victoria, had included the lighting of beacons around her realm. On the night of 3 June 2002, Elizabeth II stood in front of the Victoria Memorial on the Mall and lit a beacon that began a chain of 2,006 flames around the UK to celebrate her Golden Jubilee. Towns, cities and villages gathered to make their mark on the night sky as the pinnacle of the celebrations beckoned.

If 2002 had begun with doubts as to whether anyone would turn up to mark the half century of the Queen's reign, the morning of 4 June laid all the fears to rest. The Gold State Coach made its way through huge crowds in central London, conveying Elizabeth II and Prince Philip to St. Paul's Cathedral. The Queen and her consort looked out at a sea of flags from across the Commonwealth and, if only briefly, the famously emotionally controlled Monarch appeared to be on the brink of tears. Inside the cool marble walls of St. Paul's, she heard more tributes as the National Service of Thanksgiving for her reign took place. As the trumpeters stood to herald the national anthem, her composure once more came close to crumbling. The person behind the Crown was overcome by the emotion of the event.

At the lunch that followed at the Guildhall, her theme from earlier in the year of change had been replaced by one of calm. The Queen told fellow guests:

> Gratitude, respect and pride, these words sum up how I feel about the people of this country and the Commonwealth—and what this Golden Jubilee means to me.

Elizabeth II had begun the day in blue but switched to a bright red coat and hat for the final set piece parade of the Jubilee. She was carried along the Mall in an open top car, standing alongside Prince Philip to greet the thousands who had come to see them. They were treated to a carnival performance featuring entertainers and floats as well as 5,000 people from across the Commonwealth in their own national outfits. Her main gift that afternoon was a 'rainbow of wishes', handwritten ideals from schoolchildren across the Commonwealth.

The Queen made her way on to the balcony of Buckingham Palace with the extended Royal Family around her for a flypast featuring the Red Arrows and Concorde. And, once more, a brief glimmer of emotion was more than visible for this was a poignant moment for the Monarch. She had first stepped on to the balcony as part of 'Us Four', the affectionate name given by her father, King George VI, to his family. Now, Elizabeth was the sole remaining member of that watertight unit. She had never before celebrated a major milestone without at least one of her parents or her sister at her side. Just months after saying goodbye to her mother and to Princess Margaret, she faced the crowds, for the first time, without them. The high point of her reign so far was also a reminder of all that she had lost in the months leading up to it.

Her moment of mixed emotions was witnessed by millions. TV audiences for the Golden Jubilee were high with almost two thirds of all UK viewers tuning in for the parade down the Mall. The balcony appearance saw viewing figures peak and even highlights programmes of the day drew higher than average audiences. Meanwhile, tens of thousands had taken part in street parties and community celebrations, enjoying soggy sandwiches and fairy cakes beneath improvised bunting and flags. In some ways, this celebration of Elizabeth II looked very similar to her Silver anniversary and the Jubilees that had gone before. A nostalgia for tradition had helped as 'Cool Britannia' gave way, if only for a few days, to royal retro.

As the fold-up chairs were stacked away and the paper plates put in the recycling, the Queen continued her goodwill visits, travelling to north London, west Sussex and Wales in the seven days immediately after the main Jubilee celebrations. On 15 June she was back in London for Trooping the Colour before heading to Windsor for another showpiece event.

Queen Victoria's Golden Jubilee had begun with a huge banquet for royalty from across Europe. Elizabeth II brought the major phase of her own celebrations to a close with a replica event. On the evening of 17 June 2002, following the Garter service at St. George's Chapel, she gathered the crowned heads of Europe around her at Windsor Castle to mark her half century of rule.

None of them had held power when her historic reign had begun and she had seen all of them take their thrones. This was a moment for the history books as she took centre stage in a photo bringing together every king and queen on the continent. It was a noticeably smaller group than the one which had celebrated Victoria's Golden Jubilee and all of them had a story to tell of how their own monarchy had survived the intervening century of turbulence. At their heart sat the only one of them to have, so far, marked two major jubilees.

Even when the focal point of the celebrations was over, the Queen's work continued. She visited members of the Armed Forces and held garden parties through the summer including a special event for people who had been born on the day she became Monarch, 6 February 1952. Her tour of the UK took her to Yorkshire, the Midlands, Liverpool and East Anglia and culminated with a visit to the Edinburgh Tattoo which took on its own Jubilee theme. After her usual holiday in Balmoral, she prepared to complete her year of celebrations with a twelve-day tour of Canada.

The mood on this final leg of a worldwide journey which had seen her cover over 40,000 miles was noticeably more relaxed and jubilant than that on her earlier overseas visits. Although she found herself landing to a dissenting voice, as the Deputy Prime Minister, John Manley, said he believed Canada should become a republic just as the Monarch touched down, his opinion seemed to go against the general mood of a country that was ready to party. Thousands had attended a levee to mark the Jubilee earlier that year while the Queen Elizabeth II Golden Jubilee Medal had already been instigated, to reward those who had contributed to public life.

As she travelled from the west to the east coast of Canada, Elizabeth II was greeted by crowds leading to a spontaneous walkabout in Victoria as the Queen determined to meet the many well-wishers who had come to greet her as she left a service of thanksgiving at Christ Church Cathedral. There was plenty of royal tradition, from unveiling a new statue of herself, to planting trees as well as visits to schools, museums and the military.

But the theme of change remained constant. At the start of her visit, on 4 October 2002, she inaugurated the legislative assembly of Nunavut, the newest territory in Canada. On 6 October, she dropped the first puck at an NHL ice hockey game in Vancouver, the first time a Monarch had done the honours in Canada. A visit to the Canadian Broadcasting Corporation in Toronto saw her giggle at a film montage showing her throughout her half century of rule as Queen of Canada. Much had altered but Elizabeth II's determination to underline her commitment to the ever-evolving realms in which she reigned remained the same.

In a speech at the State Dinner given in her honour on 13 October 2002, that change was at the heart of her words. She thanked Canadians:

> ...for the loyalty, encouragement and support you have given to me over these past 50 years... your understanding

> and compassion, your confidence and engagement, are sources of inspiration to me. I would like to affirm before you tonight that wherever the future may take us, my admiration and affection for Canada and Canadians everywhere is, and will always remain, clear, strong and sure.

The visit ended with another tree planting. That year had seen her carry that duty out dozens of times as she left a lasting legacy of a celebration that had involved millions of people around the world. Even that bastion of royal power, Windsor Castle, was changed to mark this special anniversary. For the first time in nearly 200 years, a new public area at the residence was created and named, aptly, the Jubilee Gardens.

On 25 December 2002, dressed in pale blue and with photos of her parents and her sister behind her, the Queen spoke once more to her country and the Commonwealth. There was sadness for those who had marked the past festive season with her but who were now long gone from the corridors of Sandringham where the Royal Family would spend the holidays. But there was also a celebratory tone as she reflected on a Jubilee that had exceeded expectations. In an address in which she underlined her own belief in 'the long view', the Queen returned to her message of change but with a new perspective, telling her audience that the past year had been more than an anniversary and that:

> …the celebrations were joyous occasions, but they also seemed to evoke something more lasting and profound – a sense of belonging and pride in country, town or community; a sense of sharing a common heritage enriched by the cultural, ethnic and religious diversity of our 21st century society. I hope it also provided an occasion to acknowledge the progress of the past 50 years

> and the contributions of those who have done so much to make this country what it is today.

And as 2002 drew to an end, a guitarist serenading the Monarch from the top of the most famous palace in the world became one of the most abiding images of the year, twelve months that had seen Elizabeth II reign supreme as she marked her Golden Jubilee.

## Chapter Seven

# The Diamond Jubilee of Elizabeth II

At many of the major moments of the Queen's reign, the weather has been far from helpful. Her Coronation Day saw some of the heaviest rain in London for years and, almost six decades later, the skies above the capital opened once more on a spectacular celebration of her rule. As the Queen sailed down the Thames on a gilded barge, surrounded by hundreds of boats, she did it in a torrential downpour. But as Elizabeth II marked sixty years as Queen, the weather did nothing to dampen the desire of millions to mark the moment alongside her. The pageant was a huge success and provided a magnificent and moving spectacle for only the second Diamond Jubilee that Britain had ever known.

Elizabeth II's golden vessel took her along the river amidst a flotilla that ended up a record breaker. Over 3,000 vessels had been entered with organisers narrowing it down to around a thousand boats as the Jubilee date approached. They chose vessels to represent every facet of the Queen's life and reign. Some of the 'little boats' that had taken part in the Dunkirk rescues sailed alongside the royal barge. Steamboats and tugs, dinghies and dragon boats all lined up under London's grey skies on 3 June for the first major public event of this Jubilee. They were serenaded on their way by musicians on ten barges who played as they sailed, performing brand new compositions from some of Britain's most celebrated artists. Over 20,000 people were on board boats on the Thames that day to mark the third Jubilee of Elizabeth II.

The Queen herself stood under a gilded canopy on the ornately decked MV *Spirit of Chartwell*. At the front of the procession was a brand new rowing barge, inspired by royal boats of the past. The *Gloriana*, with her gold and red decorations, moved through the water ahead of the river parade while over a million people cheered from the river banks. Meanwhile, The Queen's dutiful cousin, the Duke of Kent, joined the flotilla on an RNLI lifeboat, a nod to their shared support of the lifesaving organisation, while Elizabeth II's ever practical only daughter, the Princess Royal, took to a pilot boat in front of the royal barge, leaving the glitter to those above.

It was emblematic of one of the main themes of this Diamond Jubilee. For the focus in this celebration of Elizabeth II's reign was on the Monarch herself and her immediate successors. Her son and heir, Prince Charles, had made no secret of his desire to 'slim down' the Royal Family as his own reign approached. The huge popularity of his sons, Prince William and Prince Harry, as well as of William's wife, the Duchess of Cambridge, meant much of the focus fell on the next generation any way, but this Jubilee was notable for the very pointed moves from the House of Windsor to put the spotlight on just a handful of members as an indication of changes to come.

Like many of the most famous moments of past Jubilees, the flotilla had been created by the people celebrating their Monarch's reign. This was a popular outpouring of support but it was also a demonstration of the new confidence in national identity. In 2012 there was a strong feeling of pride in Britain across many parts of the country. This was shown in the official Diamond Jubilee logo which featured the red, white and blue of the Union Jack rather than the more muted shades of sage green or burnished gold of past celebrations. For the first time, too, the UK's flag also featured prominently on the emblem which had been designed by a ten-year-old student, Katherine Dewar, following a competition on the children's TV programme, Blue Peter. Her creation, which also showed six diamonds flanking a crown, was shared without copyright and ended up on posters, biscuit tins and T-shirts across the country.

The inclusion of the 'little boats' from Dunkirk was a nod to the Queen's wartime experience as was the inclusion of a barge that had carried the coffin of Winston Churchill on its final journey. Her first Prime Minister had been an integral part of her youth as he worked alongside her father during the Second World War, but it was also another indication of the importance the military community played in this celebration. The Armed Forces have always been vital to Jubilees but in the years leading up to 2012, there had been a huge swell of support for all members of the Army, Navy and Air Force family. Conflicts in Iraq and Afghanistan and the deaths in action of those who fought there had led to widespread demonstrations of loyalty. Just a year before her Jubilee, the Queen had granted 'royal' status to the town of Wootton Bassett where local residents had spent several years forming guards of honour for repatriation of service personnel killed while fighting for their country. Among the boats that took to the Thames for the flotilla was *The Shropshire Lad* whose twelve-strong crew included eight wounded servicemen. Meanwhile the official Jubilee song that played on radios across the procession featured the voices of the Military Wives choir. This Jubilee was a celebration of more than royalty.

At its heart remained the Queen. The wet weather didn't deter Elizabeth II who, wearing diamond white, remained at the head of the procession through the unseasonably cold snap that greeted her Jubilee. She was flanked by the Duchess of Cornwall, in cream, and the Duchess of Cambridge, in bright red, while the men in the royal party wore military uniforms in blue to produce a patriotic display on the water as the national anthem was played every time they approached one of the many bridges on the route.

Prince Philip had raised a giggle from his adult grandchildren as he bobbed up and down to the music played as the pageant continued. He reprimanded them with a wry smile and continued to stand on the deck, despite the awful weather. Soon after his return to Buckingham

Palace, he was taken ill and, within hours, he was admitted to hospital with a bladder infection and missed the rest of the Jubilee weekend.

It was another indication of how times were changing but that theme that had been present in the earliest plans for this Diamond celebration. Unlike the Silver and Golden Jubilees, it had long been decided that the Queen and the Duke of Edinburgh wouldn't be the omnipresent figures of the past. Instead, major events, including all the Commonwealth tours, were passed over to younger members of the Royal Family. This Jubilee, more than any so far in the reign of Elizabeth II, was focused on the future.

As the Queen's Golden Jubilee came to an end, in 2002, there was every expectation that Elizabeth II would follow in the footsteps of Queen Victoria and celebrate the sixtieth anniversary of her reign. At the start of 2010, the UK government confirmed an extra Bank Holiday in 2012 for the occasion and moved the late May Bank Holiday as well to form the now traditional four-day long weekend for the Jubilee.

Later that same year, the Queen visited Canada and, during her stop in Ottawa, she unveiled the design of a Diamond Jubilee window which would be installed at Rideau Hall, celebrating both her reign and that of Queen Victoria. It was a seal of royal approval for a project that wouldn't be realised for another two years. Elizabeth II and those around her were clearly certain that her Diamond Jubilee would be reached, even before it had arrived, but they were also hinting that the Queen wouldn't be in Canada to mark it.

The final confirmation that the Queen and Prince Philip would confine themselves to UK visits came at the end of 2011. Buckingham Palace announced a string of Diamond Jubilee tours around the Commonwealth but none of them were to be undertaken by the Monarch and her consort. That same month, Prince Philip was taken to hospital where he was treated for a blocked coronary artery. The Diamond Jubilee was already shaping up to be very different.

One thing, however, remained the same as it had for most of the sixty years of the Queen's reign. Since the first days of her rule, Elizabeth II had preferred to spend the actual anniversary of her accession at Sandringham in Norfolk, the place where her father, King George VI, had died in the early hours of 6 February 1952. Exactly sixty years later, she spent her morning there before heading out to nearby Dersingham Infant and Nursery School where a large crowd, armed with Union Jacks and flags of St. George were on hand to greet her. She was shown a wall of children's art marking her Jubilee and also attended a grand civic reception at Kings Lynn Town Hall as her reign reached sixty years.

The day before, she had been greeted by sizeable crowds, despite the snow, as she made her way to Sunday service at West Newton church with Prince Philip, now recovered from his hospital stay, at her side. There had been another chance to see the Jubilee Queen a few days earlier when she planted a tree at the new Diamond Jubilee Wood near Sandringham with the Princess Royal.

Aware of the interest in the anniversary, the Queen's Diamond Jubilee portrait was released on the sixtieth anniversary of her accession. Taken by John Swannell, it was laden with symbolism. Elizabeth II was photographed in the Centre Room at Buckingham Palace, the spot where she and her Royal Family gather before stepping out on to the famous balcony at major events, including her Jubilees. Behind her, just slightly elevated, was the Victoria Memorial, built for the only other British Monarch to mark a Diamond Jubilee. The Queen also chose to wear the Coronation necklace and earrings which Victoria had also used for her own Diamond Jubilee portraits.

It was also a signal for the Jubilee year to begin in earnest. The Queen returned to London where her usual round of engagements and constitutional duties was amplified by Jubilee events including an interfaith conference at Lambeth Palace in the middle of February. That occasion, like every other royal event at the time, was covered extensively in the press. The Royal Family dominated the news in a good way as winter turned into spring.

Ten years earlier, there had been concerns that the Golden Jubilee would turn into a non-event as the image of the Royal Family was still recovering from a decade of damage caused by scandals, rows over money and the public backlash that followed the death of Diana, Princess of Wales. In 2012, the House of Windsor was the story everyone wanted to enjoy. The 2011 marriage of second in line to the throne, Prince William, to his university sweetheart, Catherine Middleton, had been a popular success and the newlyweds, now Duke and Duchess of Cambridge, were the most talked about couple in the world. William's younger brother, Prince Harry, had shaken off his tabloid image as a partying royal and was winning plaudits for his military role and support for service personnel. The younger generation was boosting the Monarchy's image just as the Jubilee showcased it with months of glittering events.

The focus on a new wave of Windsors had its disadvantages. Soon after the anniversary of the Queen's accession, the first Commonwealth tour for the Jubilee took place. In the earliest part of the year, the Earl and Countess of Wessex travelled to St. Lucia, Barbados, Saint Vincent and the Grenadines, Grenada, Trinidad and Tobago, Monserrat, St. Kitts and Nevis, Anguilla and Antigua and Barbuda. But the papers back home were more interested in the new duchess. With William and Catherine yet to start a family, speculation over a possible royal pregnancy sometimes took precedence over the details of these early Jubilee visits. As a consequence, the Duke of Gloucester toured the British Virgin Islands and then Malta with barely a mention.

The second wave of Commonwealth events grabbed more attention. As Edward and Sophie ended their Caribbean visits, Prince Harry arrived in Belize for his first Jubilee tour. Harry's first official visit on behalf of the Queen got plenty of attention. The prince was snapped chatting happily to children as he named a road after his grandmother, while during a trip to Jamaica he gave the press just what they wanted by posing next to superstar athlete, Usain Bolt, trying to mimic the runner's famous lightning sign. When his boat broke down during an engagement to the Bahamas and he ended up taking a lift with the press pack, his tour got even more attention. The Jubilee visits, like much of the royal focus in 2012, were proving to be all about the younger generation but they also provided a link with another landmark event set to dominate Britain in 2012.

The Summer Olympics would be held in London in July, just weeks after the Diamond Jubilee weekend with the Queen performing the official opening. The Princess Royal had been heavily involved with winning the Games for Britain during the bidding process seven years earlier. As the wait to London 2012 hit 100 days, Princess Anne was in the middle of her Jubilee tour to Mozambique. She marked the start of this final countdown at a sports academy in Boane, Maputo County. The connection between the Jubilee, the royals and the sporting event billed as the greatest show on earth was cemented.

By the time Anne took the Jubilee tours to Africa, the Queen and the Duke of Edinburgh had begun their own visits to mark the Diamond anniversary. Their itinerary around the UK would prove to be every bit as extensive as previous Jubilees but less intense, with visits spread out across months rather than packed into weeks as had happened previously.

They began their Diamond Jubilee tour in Leicester on 8 March 2012 where, in another sign of the changing image of the Royal Family, they were accompanied by the Duchess of Cambridge. The royal party arrived by train to be greeted by large crowds waving union flags. A packed day, which included a student fashion show and an inter faith reception, would be followed by a gap of almost three weeks before the next Jubilee visit, this time to Salford where the Queen opened the BBC's new base. Six days later, the tour took her and Prince Philip to Walthamstow where they were guests of honour at a lunch attended by mayors from thirty-two London boroughs.

The Queen was feted by these civic leaders just days after one of the most solemn and traditional parts of her Jubilee year. On 20 March 2012, she walked through the massed ranks of the House of Commons and the House of Lords, gathered beneath the hammerbeam roof of Westminster Hall. On a gilded chair, placed on the raised steps where her medieval predecessors had spoken to their own followers, her presence was heralded by trumpeters before, surrounded by Beefeaters, she addressed the assembled houses, telling them:

> Parliament has survived as an unshakeable cornerstone of our constitution and our way of life. History links Monarchs and Parliament, a connecting thread from one period to the next. So, in an era when the regular, worthy rhythm of life is less eye-catching than doing something extraordinary, I am reassured that I am merely the second Sovereign to celebrate a Diamond Jubilee.

There were warm words of tribute, too, for the Duke of Edinburgh as her consort sat at her side:

> Prince Philip is, I believe, well known for declining compliments of any kind. But throughout, he has been a constant strength and guide.

And she ended her address by renewing the promise she made as a twenty-one-year old, to continually serve her country, saying:

> [W]e are reminded here of our past, of the continuity of our national story and the virtues of resilience, ingenuity and tolerance which created it. I have been privileged to witness some of that history and, with the support of my family, rededicate myself to the service of our great country and its people now, and in the years to come.

Parliament's gift to the Queen for her anniversary was a stained glass window that was unveiled by Elizabeth II following her address. Featuring her Royal Arms and the words 'Diamond Jubilee', it had been paid for by personal contributions from MPs and peers in line with the Queen's wish, stated as preparations got under way for her latest milestone, that as little public money as possible be spent on the Jubilee. It was in line with earlier Jubilees, including Britain's first royal celebration for George III in 1809, where the focus had been on ensuring marking the Monarchy didn't result in a hefty bill for the people.

Another link to that first Jubilee came on 27 March 2012 when Elizabeth II, dressed in gold, received the loyal addresses of the 'privileged bodies' in a special ceremony at Buckingham Palace. In 1809, these addresses had been read across the UK before parchment versions were sent to London. George III's descendant instead sat on a gilded chair in the London palace he had bought for the Royal Family for the presentation. The Chancellors of Oxford and Cambridge Universities along with the Archbishop of Canterbury were among those offering their formally recorded wishes for the Queen's health and happiness.

The creation of new cities to mark a Jubilee had begun in Queen Victoria's time. In the spring of her Diamond Jubilee year, the Queen bestowed the honour on St. Asaph, Perth and Chelmsford which became the first ever city in Essex. She also awarded Royal Borough status to Greenwich, part of London which had long links to her ancestors and where she had carried out one of her first public engagements in 1937, helping her parents open the new National Maritime Museum.

In April 2012, she sat on board the *Cutty Sark* in its dry dock to formally oversee Greenwich's new status as well as to officially reopen the nineteenth century ship as a tourist attraction following its restoration. It was another link to the era of Victoria, the Queen who had been a constant royal reference in the run up to this

Diamond celebration. However, a nod to another renowned queen now appeared. Elizabeth II's trip to Greenwich also saw her officially unveil *Gloriana*, the specially commissioned royal barge which would lead the pageant on the Thames. Based on the Tudor rowing barges that had borne Elizabeth I along the river centuries before, and gilded to sparkle in the summer weather, it carried her royal nickname which was officially bestowed on it by Elizabeth II.

The trip to the now Royal Borough of Greenwich began a new phase of Jubilee tours for the Queen. The end of April saw her undertake a two day tour of Wales which included one of the most poignant moments of her Jubilee year. The Queen returned to Aberfan, where 144 people including 116 children, died in a landslide in 1966. It had been one of the most tragic events of her long reign and her decision to return there was seen as an important show of support to a community still in mourning.

Her trip to Wales also brought the most high profile protests about the Jubilee so far. The leader of Plaid Cymru, Leanne Wood, turned down an invitation to a service of thanksgiving for the Queen at Llandaff Cathedral while a group called Republic Wales took to social media to promote its opposition to the visit.

There were larger protests in May when the King of Bahrain was among the guests at a lunch for royalty from around the world, hosted by the Queen at Windsor Castle. King Hamid Al-Khalifa's presence came a year after the repression of anti-government protests in Bahrain. Further demonstrations took place the same evening as the Prince of Wales hosted a dinner for the visiting royals with protesters holding up signs reading 'royal dictators not welcome'.

The Queen posed for a photo with her fellow rulers at Windsor Castle but it was the images of protests that made the papers in a Jubilee that had become a media event more than any of its predecessors. It was one of the few moments of discord in the final countdown to the Diamond Jubilee weekend. The first major event of the main summer celebrations had taken place at Windsor just a few days before the protests when the Queen and the Duke of Edinburgh had attended the Diamond Jubilee Pageant which had been incorporated into the Windsor Horse Show. The pageant, telling the story of the Queen's reign with a focus on her overseas visits, featured over 1,100 performers, many of whom had been entertained at a tea party by the Queen days earlier.

On 19 May Windsor was the setting for another historic event. The three branches of the Armed Forces performed a muster and parade together for a Jubilee for the first time. The Queen and the Duke of Edinburgh took their seats in the quadrangle at Windsor Castle for a flypast by Typhoons before 2,500 members of the Army, Navy and RAF marched past. The royal party headed by car to Home Park while the military marched through the town and flag waving crowds. A final review by the Monarch brought the parade to an end. It proved to be one of the biggest popular successes of the Jubilee, tapping into the strong wave of support for the military at the time.

Some of the Jubilee celebrations at the Chelsea Flower Show on 21 May 2012 were more down to earth with the Queen being shown vegetables grown to mark her milestone as she toured generation gardens as well as special floral displays spelling out the years of her Jubilee. Less than twenty-four hours later, Elizabeth II was welcoming thousands to Buckingham Palace for the first of her summer garden parties. The following evening saw her feted by some of the biggest names in showbusiness as Joan Collins and Shirley Bassey led tributes at a Jubilee evening at the Royal Academy of Arts.

It provided stand out photos for a Jubilee that was more media led than any of its predecessors. Since the Golden celebrations of 2002, the rise of social media had seen millions sign up to Facebook and Twitter, among them the Royal Family themselves. Selling this Jubilee was all about a great picture and that focus on image became clear as there was huge interest in a giant representation of the Queen at her Silver celebrations in 1977 that was draped across Sea Containers House on the River Thames in the days before the Diamond Jubilee weekend. Artist Chris Devine produced the first hologram portrait of the Queen which was unveiled as May 2012 came to an end, topped with a diamond replica of the George IV Diadem she had worn on her way to her Coronation. Image was everything.

Image also informed the Jubilee stamps which went on sale as the weekend celebrations approached. The Royal Mail chose eight photos of the Queen for the special set, including one from her Golden Jubilee and another from her Silver celebrations. An unusual photo from 1957, taken as she addressed the General Assembly of the United Nations, was selected to underline her position as a Head of State as well as hereditary Monarch.

The profusion of royal stories meant that the visit of the Prince of Wales and the Duchess of Cornwall to Canada in the last days of May was somewhat overshadowed. The couple visited the provinces of New Brunswick, Ontario and Saskatchewan between 21 and 25 May 2012 but their tour took second place to the glittering events in the UK. However, the involvement of Prince Charles in an event to honour the military, an ongoing theme of this Jubilee, drew widespread attention as May came to an end.

The Prince of Wales presented the Queen's Diamond Jubilee medal to twenty-eight members of the Victoria and George Cross Association including Johnson Beharry who had been awarded the VC for his bravery in Iraq in 2005. This special ceremony was another reminder of the significant role given to the military in this Diamond Jubilee. In total, over 450,000 members of the Armed Forces, emergency services and the Prison Service who had five years or more service on 6 February 2012 would be presented with the medal. The design, by Timothy Noad, followed the tradition of Jubilee medals and showed the Queen's cypher and the dates of her reign on a diamond shape. Members of the Royal Household also received the medal, in line with past Jubilees.

This high profile recognition of the military came just as the main Jubilee weekend got under way. As celebrations began, it was confirmed by Parliament that the tower that housed Big Ben would be renamed in honour of the Queen. The Elizabeth Tower stands at the opposite end of the Palace of Westminster to the Victoria Tower which had been renamed for the first Diamond Queen in 1897. As this historic decision was revealed, the Queen and the Duke of Edinburgh were on their way to the Epsom Derby with two of their granddaughters, Princess Beatrice and Princess Eugenie.

The following day, the whole Royal Family was in attendance at the Thames Diamond Jubilee Pageant, taking up berths in different ships as the country celebrated the Queen with an Elizabethan-style river show that sailed from Wandsworth to Tower Bridge. The Guinness Book of World Records gave Elizabeth II another place in the history books as it confirmed this celebration of her reign was the largest ever parade of boats.

As well as those that formed the actual procession, hundreds more took part in an Avenue of Sail along the riverside. Amongst its numbers were ships too large to pass under some of London's famous bridges including *Amazon*, a yacht that took part in celebrations for Queen Victoria's Diamond Jubilee, and *Suhali*, the boat that made Sir Robin Johnston-Knox a record breaker when he sailed it around the world in 1969. The *Matthew of Bristol*, a replica of the ship that took John Cabot to North America, also joined the Avenue. They took their place alongside warships, oyster smackers and eel barges as a guard of honour for the main parade.

As the Queen's boat, the MV *Spirit of Chartwell*, prepared to join the flotilla, a group of fifty-five dinghies, each bearing the flag of a Commonwealth country, sailed on before her. Around the royal boat, in pride of place, were forty-five little boats from Dunkirk which would make their way past the MTB102 which Churchill and Eisenhower had used exactly seventy-eight years before to inspect the D-Day fleet. And spreading out behind, in a huge fan, were hundreds more vessels including motorboats from yacht clubs around the country, working fireboats, canal barges and a duckboat.

The Queen stood beneath a golden canopy, surrounded by flowers, on her barge which had been painted red, purple and gold for the occasion. Its lower decks were draped with red velvet while the stern carried a gilded figure of Old Father Time. The Royal Philharmonic Orchestra had sailed down the river playing music associated with famous buildings on the route while the Ancient Academy of Music had been on another barge, performing Handel's Water Music on eighteenth-century instruments. A waterborne bell tower had been built on a reinforced barge that sailed along, chiming a quarter peel on eight bells cast for the Jubilee and named after members of the Royal Family. The whole event had been designed to produce a spectacular view of the Jubilee Queen for the crowds that gathered. Organisers estimated more than a million people watched the flotilla from the banks of the Thames.

They, like the Royal Family, were chilled through as the royal barge finally sailed under Tower Bridge to another burst of 'God Save The Queen'. The Prince of Wales had taken a back seat in the royal party with the Queen and the Duke of Edinburgh at the heart of the celebrations and the Duke and Duchess of Cambridge at the centre of media interest. However, within hours, Prince Philip had become unwell and on the morning of 4 June he was admitted to hospital. Prince Charles now stepped up to escort his mother through the main events of her Diamond Jubilee.

The sudden illness of the Duke of Edinburgh came as a shock and caused widespread worry. He was about to celebrate his ninety-first birthday and although he had recovered well from treatment for heart problems just months earlier, his health gave cause for concern. Buckingham Palace played down the illness and stated clearly that the Queen would continue with her Jubilee plans. It was left to the Earl and Countess of Wessex to take on the hospital visits with Prince Edward telling reporters his father was watching the celebrations on television.

Meanwhile, Prince Charles was on hand to welcome his mother to the stage built around the Victoria Memorial as she joined him at the end of the special concert put on outside Buckingham Palace on the evening of 4 June 2012. The Golden Jubilee concerts had been huge successes and the decision to hold another at the Palace in 2012 led to a rush for tickets. The ballot for places was open for a month at the start of 2012 and over 1.2 million people applied for the 10,000 places at the event. The recipients, drawn by ballot, were also welcomed into the Palace gardens ahead of the concert for a picnic created for them by Heston Blumenthal and Mark Flanagan. As evening began to fall, they took their places for the concert which featured some of the biggest music stars in the world including Tom Jones, Elton John, Kylie Minogue and Paul McCartney.

The theme of support for the Armed Forces community was also on show at the concert as the official Jubilee anthem was performed by the Military Wives choir alongside its composer, Gary Barlow. Up to 500,000 people heard its already familiar tune float along the Mall as they watched the concert on the giant screens put up there and in the Royal Parks for those who didn't get tickets in the ballot. The song would go on to reach number one.

The Queen attended the last part of the concert, having handed over the main place in the royal box to her son and heir and while a rendition of 'God Save the Queen' had become the iconic moment of the Golden Jubilee concert, it was the Prince of Wales who provided the star turn at the follow up. In a speech which clearly left the Queen moved, he paid tribute to her dedication and service and got one of the biggest reactions of the evening when he addressed her as 'Your Majesty, Mummy'. As he led the crowd in three cheers for the Jubilee Queen, a huge Union Jack was projected on to Buckingham Palace while the Mall, filled to capacity, resounded with noise and more waving flags. The Queen went on to light the Jubilee beacon which set off a chain of torches and bonfires across the UK and the Commonwealth while fireworks lit up the roof of her famous London home. It was a spectacular sight which fitted the Jubilee image to perfection.

Since George III marked the first royal Jubilee in Britain over two hundred years earlier, a Service of Thanksgiving had been a crucial part of all commemorations. On 5 June 2012, the last day of her Jubilee weekend, the Queen travelled to St. Paul's Cathedral for a ceremony marking her long reign. Prince Charles took the seat next to his mother for the service which was attended by the whole Royal Family.

A carriage procession back to Buckingham Palace saw the Queen ask the Duchess of Cornwall to sit at her side, taken as a statement of support for Camilla who had suffered from criticism following her wedding to the Prince of Wales given their relationship during his first marriage. But back at base, the wider family was left indoors. Prince Charles had made it clear in the years before the Jubilee that his vision for the House of Windsor under his stewardship was a slimline Monarchy, focussed on just a handful of royals. The final, crowning moment of this Jubilee, the balcony appearance at Buckingham Palace, saw the Queen surrounded by just five royals. Along with the Prince of Wales and the Duchess of Cornwall, the Duke and Duchess of Cambridge and Prince Harry appeared to acknowledge the huge crowds. It was a clear mark of support from Elizabeth II for her heir's future plans.

It drew criticism, however, with less enthusiastic commentators saying it left the Royal Family looking depleted at the moment of its greatest glory. For there was no doubt that the Jubilee weekend had been a huge success. Millions had converged on London while the reception given to the Royal Family had been as positive as any in their recent history. The House of Windsor was positioned firmly at the heart of national life once more. The Queen's beaming smile as she left King Edward VII Hospital after visiting her husband seemed to indicate that even the most worrying aspect of this Jubilee would have a happy ending.

Despite the main celebrations being over, the traditional events of summer were all given a special Jubilee touch. The surge in popularity that the Royal Family had enjoyed after the Jubilee party were seen in the larger than usual crowds that packed Windsor for the Order of the Garter parade and the big turnouts as Jubilee visits began again.

The Queen headed to Nottingham on 14 June with the Duke and Duchess of Cambridge accompanying her while Prince Philip continued to recuperate. The Queen planted a tree next to one set in place by Queen Victoria for her own Diamond Jubilee while Prince William paid tribute to his grandmother, saying '*how grateful we are for the extraordinary love and devotion you have shown the people of this country and the Commonwealth'*.

Prince Philip was back in action soon after his birthday and presented his wife with the Queen's Cup when her horse triumphed in that race at Royal Ascot as June came to an end. He was also at her side for her Jubilee visit to Northern Ireland which saw her shake hands with Sinn Fein's Martin McGuinness in a much anticipated meeting.

The Queen's visit to Belfast and Enniskillen came during one of the most intense parts of her Jubilee visits. Between 13 June and 25 July, she clocked up sixteen days of tours, taking her from Scotland to the Isle of Wight and from Stevenage to Gateshead. A Commonwealth visit to Gibraltar by the Earl and Countess of Wessex, at the same time, ran into controversy when a Spanish minister called their presence on the disputed territory an affront.

However, the world was about to look to London again and, despite a lack of official Jubilee links, the show they saw became part of a triumphant summer for the Royal Family. On 27 July 2012, a global audience of 900 million people watched Elizabeth II open the London Olympics. As Head of State, it was expected that the Queen would oversee the official beginning of this sporting spectacular. The ceremony, directed by Oscar winning film director Danny Boyle, was another triumph of a new pride in national awareness but its most famous moment came from Elizabeth II. In a move that took the world by surprise, the Queen appeared in a spoof James Bond sketch, alongside Daniel Craig, which saw her head out of Buckingham Palace and pretend to parachute into the Opening Ceremony before walking on to the biggest cheer of the night. The Jubilee Queen had stolen the show and the Royal Family's popularity soared even higher.

The later part of the year would continue the success of the Diamond celebrations. In September 2012, the Duke and Duchess of Cambridge carried out a hugely popular tour of Singapore, Malaysia, Tuvalu and the Solomon Islands. It attracted huge attention as the Duchess made her first public speech overseas, showing her support for the hospice movement. The couple were photographed dancing while decked with floral garlands and, more controversially, being carried through crowds on the backs of elephants. There was controversy, too, as a French magazine published paparazzi shots of the Duchess, topless, leading to the couple taking legal action which they later won.

Meanwhile, the Queen's year continued to fill with Jubilee events. In October 2012, she confirmed she would honour universities around the UK with Regius Professorships to recognise excellence in research. Six would be chosen, one for each decade of her reign.

The visit to Australia and New Zealand by the Prince of Wales and the Duchess of Cornwall in November 2012 rounded off the year of tours with the couple spending time in Queensland, Victoria, South Australia and New South Wales before heading to Auckland, Wellington, Christchurch and Manawatu. Soon after they landed back in the UK, came the perfect royal ending to the perfect royal year. The Duke and Duchess of Cambridge announced their were expecting their first child. Their baby would guarantee the succession into the twenty-second century.

Amidst the triumphs of her Jubilee year, the Queen had also given assent to laws that changed the rules on who could inherit her throne.

Boys no longer outranked girls, the Crown would pass according to order of birth, not gender.

As she reflected on 2012 in her Christmas Speech, the Queen spoke of her surprise at how many people wanted to mark the milestone, saying:

> The enthusiasm which greeted the Diamond Jubilee was, of course, especially memorable for me and my family. It was humbling that so many chose to mark the anniversary of a duty which passed to me sixty years ago. People of all ages took the trouble to take part in various ways and in many nations. But perhaps most striking of all was to witness the strength of fellowship and friendship among those who had gathered together on these occasions.

The ongoing themes of this Jubilee, of a new sense of nationality and of gratitude to those who served, was also evident in the Christmas broadcast:

> Prince Philip and I were joined by our family on the River Thames as we paid tribute to those who have shaped the United Kingdom's past and future as a maritime nation, and welcomed a wonderful array of craft, large and small, from across the Commonwealth. On the barges and the bridges and the banks of the river there were people who had taken their places to cheer through the mist, undaunted by the rain. That day there was a tremendous sense of common determination to celebrate triumphing over the elements. That same spirit was in evidence from the moment the Olympic flame arrived on these shores. The flame…was carried by every kind of deserving individual, many nominated for their own extraordinary service.

As her Jubilee year drew to a close, another attribute of this commemoration was spoken of by the Queen. The focus on the military had been striking and well supported and she ended her year with solemn words of remembrance:

> For many, Christmas is also a time for coming together. But for others, service will come first. Those serving in our Armed Forces, in our Emergency Services and in our hospitals, whose sense of duty takes them away from family and friends, will be missing those they love. And those who have lost loved ones may find this day especially full of memories.

Many memories had been created throughout the year as the Diamond Jubilee proved to be a triumph for the Royal Family. For the first time in decades, the Queen had found herself at the head of a harmonious and happy house and there was little to distract from the celebratory tone of a royal anniversary decades in the making. The focus on the future had been cemented by the royal baby news that dominated as December 2012 came to an end while the Queen's own determination to showcase the next generation at a celebration of her own achievement had left the Windsors stronger than at any time in recent memory. The Diamond Jubilee would prove to be the most successful of all Elizabeth II's celebrations, a sparkling moment in an historic reign.

# Chapter Eight

# Exporting Jubilees

As the Duke and Duchess of Cambridge were greeted by the Prime Minister of Jamaica during the first Platinum Jubilee tour of 2022, they were told directly that the chances of them ruling as King and Queen of that island were slim. Their host, Andrew Holness, began their meeting, in front of the world's media, with a statement that his country was 'moving on' and was ready to 'fulfil our true ambitions… as an independent, developed, prosperous country'. Their Jubilee visit provoked controversial debate, but exporting Jubilees had never been easy for Britain's royals.

It had been an area that caused some unease for the organisers of the very first royal anniversary celebrations. In the years before his Golden Jubilee, George III had rejected the suggestion that he take the title of Emperor of the British and Hanoverian Dominions but as preparations for his Jubilee began to pick up pace, the inclusion of his overseas realms became an area of concern. In June 1809, an extravagant celebration was held in Mumbai on the King's birthday. British representatives from across India were invited to a 'fete' marking the anniversary which included the obligatory feasting and fireworks. It was deemed a great success by those who sent back stories from the celebrations, but the general reception in India wasn't spoken of. Instead, the loyal service of the King's colonies became an important element in telling the Jubilee story to his subjects back in Britain. For those who wanted this royal festival to succeed, it was another indication of royal popularity. The sceptics saw it as an imposition. In the intervening centuries, little has changed.

The Jubilees of Elizabeth II have placed a prominent focus on including the Commonwealth. Each of her anniversary celebrations included large scale tours. However taking Jubilees overseas proved contentious even for a monarch as well travelled as Elizabeth II.

From the very earliest days of her record breaking reign, the Queen had been determined to visit as many parts of the Commonwealth as possible. As she prepared for her first Jubilee, that remained a priority. In 1977, Elizabeth II and the Duke of Edinburgh began their Jubilee visits overseas. In February, they travelled to Samoa, Tonga and Fiji before heading to New Zealand where the Queen officially opened a new session of parliament. However, not everyone welcomed her to the country. The 1960s had seen a string of countries remove the Queen as head of state and debate raged elsewhere about how long her rule would last outside Britain. During her stay in New Zealand, she encountered protests including a large demonstration demanding the withdrawal of British troops from Northern Ireland.

This Jubilee visit was her fifth tour, as Queen, of New Zealand and it was closely followed by the sixth visit of her reign to Australia. Elizabeth II spent most of March in the country, opening parliament, as well as visiting Perth, Tasmania and Sydney. Tens of thousands turned out to see her on her different stops.

She had had more of a presence in the two nations than any of her predecessors which was shown in the way the Jubilee was marked there. As well as obvious tributes such as special stamps and coins, Australia celebrated the anniversary with a touring train which took a whole host of royal artefacts, including Princess Anne's wedding dress, on a journey of several thousand miles. Over four months, it visited twenty-six stations and brought the royal story to thousands of people. Special Honours lists for the Jubilee were issued in both Australia and New Zealand while the Jubilee medal was also issued in both countries. The same pattern was followed in Canada which received a royal visit at the end of 1977.

Elizabeth II spent the majority of the first three months of her Silver Jubilee year overseas before returning for a busy set of UK engagements. Most of October 1977 was also spent taking her celebrations around the Commonwealth. As well as the trip to Canada, which saw her gifted a horse by the Mounties, she also spent time in the Bahamas, Antigua and Barbuda, Barbados and Mustique. There were state aspects to these trips as well as festivities with the Queen opening parliament in both Canada and the Bahamas.

The pattern of topping and tailing her Jubilee years with Commonwealth visits stuck for the later anniversary celebrations of Elizabeth II, but exporting her celebrations didn't get any easier. The Queen took the Jubilee to Jamaica at the start of 2002, arriving in mid February despite having just lost her only sister, Princess Margaret. Her time in the country, which included meetings with Jamaican veterans of the First World War, was followed by a difficult start to her visit to New Zealand where a fresh debate about whether the country should become a republic was in full swing, fuelled by remarks from the Prime Minister just ahead of the royal trip that cutting the Monarchy loose was all but inevitable. Prince Philip's comments during a five day visit to Australia, questioning an Aboriginal elder on whether he threw spears, led to more rows.

The tours were covered in the British press but with little enthusiasm. Photos of the Queen at a corgi show in Adelaide put on for her celebrations made the papers but not necessarily the front pages. However, the visit proved popular with a crowd of over 30,000 turning out for the last engagements in Brisbane. The Queen returned home to another sadness as her mother's health deteriorated rapidly. The Queen Mother's death, on 30 March 2002, came after a busy time for her daughter who had spent most of the last weeks away from home.

The end of the year saw the Queen travel to Canada where she spent almost two weeks. During her visit, she opened the new legislative assembly of Nunavut in Northern Canada and became the first reigning Monarch to drop the puck at an ice hockey match. By then, the success of the Jubilee celebrations in June had quelled protests at her rule which were limited to minor demonstrations in

Quebec. As at the Silver Jubilee, Canada issued its own medal while a special honours list had also marked the event.

By the time of the Diamond Jubilee, the Queen had slowed her pace of international travel dramatically and a decision was taken for the Commonwealth tours to be undertaken by other members of the Royal Family. That, in itself, caused some controversy as it took the Monarch out of the heart of these monarchical celebrations in her other realms. However, it also removed the Queen from some of the more contentious parts of these celebrations and may, as a result, have increased her popularity in her Jubilee year. The row that broke out in Gibraltar, as the celebrations were taken there, involved her youngest son, Prince Edward, and his wife, the Countess of Wessex, who turned up to oversee the festivities just as the British ambassador in Madrid was told by the Spanish Foreign Office that it was 'upset' by the visit.

A Jubilee without the Queen was a strange suggestion for countries including Canada, Australia and New Zealand which, by then, had developed regular patterns of celebrations that were inspired, but not dictated, by the UK festivities. In 2012, they still issued Jubilee stamps, coins and medals and arranged celebratory events including levees, but the main royal presence came in the form of Elizabeth II's heir.

The Queen had always proved popular and had seen off challenges to her throne, including a high profile referendum in Australia between her Silver and Golden Jubilees which had seen a majority vote in favour of retaining her as Head of State. However her heir, Prince Charles, didn't enjoy the same levels of popularity. The decision to send him and his second wife, the Duchess of Cornwall, on the highest profile Jubilee tours was a conscious decision to bolster their role in the future of the House of Windsor.

Charles and Camilla toured Canada for five days at the end of May 2012, visiting New Brunswick, Ontario and Saskatchewan. There was an autumn tour of Australia, too, for the future king whose itinerary for the Diamond Jubilee also took in New Zealand and Papua New Guinea. But the interest in these royal visits was muted in comparison to the response for tours carried out by Charles' sons.

September 2012 saw the Duke and Duchess of Cambridge head to Singapore, Malaysia, the Solomon Islands and Tuvalu with every moment of the tour eagerly covered and big crowds turning out for the new stars of the House of Windsor. The soaring popularity of William and Kate, along with an almost obsessive media interest in the clothes chosen by the new duchess, led to acres of coverage in UK papers. The tour came after a spectacularly successful summer which had seen the Royal Family feted during Diamond Jubilee celebrations and at the London Olympics where they were a constant presence.

Earlier in the year, a visit by Prince Harry to Belize, the Bahamas and Jamaica had been keenly followed. Harry, whose reputation as a party prince had made the papers in the years before, was now a solid soldier, unafraid to share his now refined charisma with dancing and discreet jokes.

Ten years later, the same tours would prove problematic as the attitude to the Monarchy in the area had changed dramatically. The Duke and Duchess of Cambridge flew into Belize to find their first engagement cancelled after protests from local residents over land claims made by a charity of which William was patron. Ahead of their arrival in Jamaica, a fierce debate raged about whether the island should follow the path of Barbados which had declared itself a republic just months earlier, dispensing with the long reign of Elizabeth II in just a few hours. The Prime Minister's confirmation to the Duke of Cambridge that he intended to move his nation towards a Crown-free future was followed by a speech from the prince in which he called slavery 'abhorrent'. Exporting the Platinum Jubilee ran into problems almost as soon as it began.

Marking celebrations in countries that had once been part of the royal realm was another issue that proved problematic as the Elizabethan Jubilees continued. In 2012, the Duke of York had carried out a brief visit to India. However, the nation wasn't included in a list of visits for 2022 while Prince Andrew had been removed from public royal life following a civil court case.

India had played a large part in Britain's first royal jubilees. In 1935, George V became the first ruler to mark a quarter of a century as Emperor of India as well as King. Special stamps and coins were issued in India but British rule there was under increasing pressure. Just five years earlier, Mahatma Gandhi had undertaken the Salt March, walking to the sea to create salt in defiance of British rule. Thousands had followed his lead, creating the first large scale protest against the power of the Empire ruled by George V.

The government of 1897 had taken a conscious decision to make Queen Victoria's Diamond Jubilee a celebration of her role, and that of Britain, at the heart of a global empire. Jubilee Day, 21 June 1897, was declared a bank holiday in India as well as Britain while Indian troops played a major part in the huge procession that made its way through London to celebrate the Queen. Officers from the Indian Imperial Service Troops went ahead of the Sovereign's escort while India's premier had taken his place among the group of eleven colonial leaders who set off at the head of the great procession that would convey Victoria to St. Paul's Cathedral. Indian cavalry had escorted her through the same streets ten years earlier when she marked her Golden Jubilee. Inside Westminster Abbey, she was joined by many Indian princes who made such an impression on American author, Mark Twain, who was observing the celebrations that he noted them down as 'men of stately build and princely carriage'.

Although Victoria hadn't been keen on the idea of Jubilee celebrations, she had been instrumental in including as much of her Indian empire in them as possible. Controversially now, that had included asking for two Indian servants to be sent to her to look after her for the duration of her Jubilee year. One of them, Abdul Karim, would become hugely influential in the Queen's later life. Although often represented as some kind of guru, his work with Victoria, which included teaching her Urdu, underlined the often discreet political role taken by the Queen who had a far greater involvement in the issues of the day than she liked to be known.

In fact, her first Jubilee had been designed to reintroduce her to her country and to her empire after the long years of seclusion that had followed her widowhood. The death of Prince Albert in December 1861 is generally given as a reason for Queen Victoria not marking a Silver Jubilee. The twenty-fifth anniversary of her reign fell in June 1862, just six months after the loss of her husband, and strict court mourning rules would have made any kind of festivity impossible. However, there was nothing to indicate that Victoria planned a major celebration. The pattern set in her grandfather's reign had been to mark the anniversary at the start of the Jubilee year. Her own twenty-fifth year had begun on 20 June 1861 when Albert was still in apparent good health. That date came and went without any festivities. Whether a major celebration would have occurred in 1862 had Albert still been alive remains a 'what if' of history. But a royal interest in jubilees was starting to take hold across Europe by then and several of her continental contemporaries had decided to celebrate their quarter centuries of rule.

In 1843, just six years after Victoria became Queen, the King of Sweden reached the twenty-fifth anniversary of his accession. King Karl XIV Johan marked his milestone with a gala performance at the Royal Swedish Opera House and a huge ball for the bourgeoisie at the Stock Exchange. The Governor of Stockholm led the welcoming committee with dignitaries from around Sweden supporting him. The King was so overwhelmed by the party that he later said he 'would rather have died' than leave his Jubilee ball.

Public involvement in this jubilee, however, was limited. Large crowds turned out to catch a glimpse of the King and Queen on their way to the ball and Te Deums were held in churches across his realm on the morning of the anniversary. But the popular festivities that had been so integral to George III's Golden Jubilee were missing.

However, the Swedish celebrations did have something in common with the British ones. King Karl XIV Johan had had to fight to shore up his royal regime. A relative by marriage of Napoleon, he'd been elected as heir to the throne during the wars that had provided such a dramatic backdrop to the first British royal jubilee. He'd gone on to be a successful King but his popularity had waned in the years before his jubilee. The celebrations acted as a confirmation of his place, and that of his Monarchy, at the heart of Swedish politics.

In the year that Queen Victoria marked her Diamond anniversary, Sweden held another Jubilee and it had a rather familiar air about it. Oskar II was celebrating twenty-five years as King, having taken the throne on 18 September 1872. However, the fanciful romanticism of Karl Johan's celebrations had been replaced with an almost identical version of a British Jubilee.

In an echo of the pattern set in 1809, these celebrations began with church services followed by the reading and presentation of loyal addresses. Just as George III had been regaled with compliments over his wisdom and honour at the start of the century, and Queen Victoria had twice found herself feted for her many royal talents, so King Oskar now found praise heaped upon him with everything written down on parchment scrolls and presented to him as a further expression of public adoration. The desire to spread this confirmation of regal beneficence far and wide found expression in printed copies of the loyal addresses being sold and circulated, just as they had been in Britain.

The later part of the celebrations was almost a direct copy of one of the most talked about parts of George III's Jubilee. The centre of Stockholm was decked out in illuminations with buildings, bridges and monuments sparkling in the evening air as King Oskar and his queen, Sophia, drove around inspecting them. Crowds gathered to party together, echoing the communal elements of British jubilees. However the big change in this Swedish jubilee was the appearance of charity and remission as an integral feature. A national collection was held in honour of King Oskar's anniversary with over 227,000 people contributing. They raised 2.2 million kroner which the monarch decided to put towards a fund to combat tuberculosis. His charitable foundation is still at work today.

It was in line with the British Jubilee practice of ensuring that anniversary celebrations supported those most in need. However, economic concerns of a different kind would ensure Oskar's son and successor, Gustaf V, missed his silver anniversary in 1932 as a financial crash that year made celebrations untenable. Two years earlier, his relative, King Haakon VII of Norway, had marked his own quarter of a century as Monarch with a low key Jubilee that gathered a smattering of royalty in Oslo for a gala concert and dinner.

Haakon, whose wife Maud was a younger sister of King George V, also issued a Jubilee medal for his silver celebrations and repeated the gesture in 1950 when he reached a half century of rule. His son, Olav V, added another medal to the Jubilee history of Norway when his silver festivities came round in 1982. Those celebrations also saw commemorative stamps and books issued.

By the time Olav's son, Harald V, reached his Silver Jubilee in 2016, the festivities had a very familiar feel. Harald and his wife, Sonja, carried out Jubilee visits across Norway while the weekend of their anniversary, in January 2016, saw them open up the doors of the Royal Palace in Oslo for a winter sports festival, free to everyone. By the time they walked to a special service at the end of their Jubilee weekend, their approval ratings were close to ninety per cent, while huge crowds cheered them through Oslo.

King Carl XVI Gustaf of Sweden has also expanded anniversary celebrations in the twentieth and twenty-first centuries. His Silver Jubilee, in 1998, saw over 2,000 people from across the country invited to a reception at the Royal Palace in Stockholm on National Day, while another communal celebration was held on the anniversary of his accession, 15 September 1998.

In 2013, he marked his fortieth anniversary with a series of Jubilee tours all around Sweden followed by a weekend of festivities which included a church service and a day of national celebrations called 'Dancing at the Palace' when people from around Sweden were invited to head to Stockholm where the royal gates were opened for people to party with their King. Meanwhile, gifts were declined with the King asking people to donate, instead, to one of his foundations in support of others. As Elizabeth II marked her Platinum Jubilee, the King of Sweden was already looking ahead to his own Golden celebrations in 2023, launching a nationwide competition to design an emblem for the party, another echo of traditions established in Britain for royal anniversaries.

In the Netherlands, the organising committee established to run the Silver Jubilee of Queen Beatrix in 2005 was explicit in its focus. The celebrations were designed as a party 'for, by and involving all the inhabitants' of the country. As with the very earliest royal jubilees, the festivities were to be generated and enjoyed by everyone. In fact, the organisers insisted that this was more a celebration of the role of Monarch rather than Beatrix herself. The date of her accession, 30 April, had been kept as Queen's Day ever since and was already an annual celebration. It became the focal point of communal celebrations for her Jubilee. However, the queen still carried out a tour of her realms to mark the quarter century while a special stamp and coin were also issued.

Her grandmother, Queen Wilhelmina, had celebrated two Jubilees, but at unexpected times. She had ascended the throne in 1890 at the age of ten and her mother, Emma, had ruled as regent until 1898 when the young queen was finally sworn in. Wilhelmina didn't mark the quarter century of her reign until 1923, when she had actually ruled by herself for twenty-five years. A week of festivities was planned with Amsterdam decked in flags and lights to mark the occasion. The Silver Jubilee of Queen Wilhelmina began with a church service followed by days of receptions and appearances at public events. In 1938, souvenirs were issued to mark Wilhelmina's Ruby Jubilee, even though she had actually been monarch for closer to fifty years.

Wilhelmina marked her Golden Jubilee in 1948, fifty years after being sworn in as Queen but nearly sixty after ascending the throne, but it also acted as a swansong. The queen had decided to abdicate some months earlier, owing to poor health, and so turned the festivities for her anniversary into a final farewell and a chance to boost the Monarchy as her daughter, Juliana, prepared to take over. Again, days of celebrations were planned, culminating in a car procession through Amsterdam and a balcony appearance which saw tens of thousands of people cheer and sing in tribute to their queen. The communal aspect of a Jubilee remained all important.

That was reflected in plans for the Golden celebrations of a monarch who has marked the most high profile Jubilees outside of Britain. In January 2022, just days before Elizabeth II's Platinum festivities, Queen Margrethe II of Denmark reached the fiftieth anniversary of her reign. She had had to postpone many of the planned events because of the Coronavirus pandemic but insisted on putting her people at the heart of her limited celebrations, even if they were socially distanced.

On 14 January 2022, when she had reigned for exactly fifty years, Margrethe took the train with her sister, her two sons and their wives to Roskilde. They were to visit the grave of her father, King Frederik IX, whose unexpected death in 1972 had propelled her to the throne, but before they got there, they made sure they were seen by as many people as possible. Authorities had asked crowds not to gather because of pandemic restrictions, however, groups had sprung up along the train route while others lined the route to the cathedral. Margrethe left her royal car to get as close to them as restrictions would allow. Even in the strangest of times, popular celebration remained vital to her Jubilee.

Margrethe was used to huge popular festivities for her Jubilees. Her ruby anniversary, in 2012, had been marked with a dramatic official emblem and a spectacular portrait which was displayed on a banner on the balcony of Copenhagen Town Hall as she stood to acknowledge a huge crowd, just one of several mass turnouts to mark her anniversary. The official events for the Jubilee included a church service, a tribute in parliament and a parade through her capital which was decorated for the occasion. Margrethe also held a glittering banquet for the crowned heads of Europe.

It followed a similar pattern to her Silver celebrations in 1997 when large crowds had gathered to cheer her through the streets of Copenhagen and her mother, Queen Ingrid, had stolen the show with an impromptu speech at the Jubilee banquet which had left many in tears. Margrethe marked her Jubilees with medals while her country paid tribute with special stamps and coins. By the time her Golden Jubilee arrived, in 2022, the importance of major celebrations in placing royalty at the heart of Danish life was underlined as Margrethe's family also put on major events to mark the fiftieth birthday of the country's Crown Princess, Mary. Exhibitions and events around both anniversaries opened as restrictions began to ease while Mary's Foundation, focused on young people, became a beneficiary of gifts sent for the royal celebrations, again putting a focus on regal events benefitting all.

Mary and her husband, Crown Prince Frederik, may well celebrate a Jubilee of their own when the throne of Denmark passes to them. Elsewhere in Europe, the practice of marking these monarchical milestones isn't as well practised. In Spain, the twenty-fifth anniversary of the accession of King Juan Carlos involved a special ceremony at the country's parliament, the Cortes, but it was a more low key celebration. Juan Carlos had taken the throne on the death of the Fascist dictator, Francisco Franco, and had helped guide his country to democracy in the years afterwards. The anniversary was as much a reflection on the huge changes that the whole country had experienced as a celebration of the Monarchy.

In Belgium, King Baudouin had taken the throne in 1951 in difficult circumstances after his father, Leopold III, had been forced to abdicate. His own reign had been a success and marked by his deep faith. He took the religious aspect of Jubilees as his main focus when his reign reached twenty-five years and established the King

Baudouin Foundation which aimed to improve the lives of many around his kingdom.

However, Jubilees can be discarded, too. When Baudouin died in 1993, his throne passed to his younger brother, Albert. In 2013, initial plans to mark the twentieth anniversary of his rule were taking shape when he surprised the whole country, and some politicians, by revealing he wouldn't be marking a jubilee at all but abdicating instead. The early summer saw him on farewell visits around Belgium, rather than Jubilee tours, and he handed over the throne to his elder son, Philippe, just weeks before his rule would have reached twenty years. Belgium got a new king and a jubilee that never was.

The decision of kings, including Albert of the Belgians and Gustaf V of Sweden, not to mark these milestones in their reign is an indication of the role of jubilees to royal families. They are opportunities to celebrate the importance of a Monarchy in national life and both men judged that their country's focus was elsewhere when their landmarks approached. Albert's abdication allowed his royal family to reinvent itself. He handed over power on Belgium's national day, 21 July, which was already a holiday and which, for years, had been a time for people to come together and celebrate. The ruling dynasty attached itself to an established celebration to re-root itself in national life rather than try and create another festivity. Belgium began the day with a monarch in his late seventies with a series of question marks over his personal life. It went to sleep under the rule of a new king with a young family, already more popular than the regime that went before.

Jubilees are about reinvention and national sentiment. For that reason, they don't always travel well outside the country where they are being celebrated. However, the record breaking nature of Elizabeth II's reign, as well as the much higher profile of her royal dynasty on a global level, has ensured that interest in Britain's royal Jubilees comes from all corners of the world.

In 2002, the Mayor of New York, Michael Bloomberg, oversaw a special tribute for the Queen's Golden Jubilee when the top of the Empire State Building was lit up in purple and gold in her honour. However, it wasn't just Jubilee sentiment that had led to the celebration. City officials said they were still overwhelmed with gratitude after the Queen had the US national anthem played at Changing the Guard to show her support for the city just hours after the Twin Towers attacks left thousands dead on 11 September 2001.

In the run up to the Platinum Jubilee of 2022, there was a specific focus on the tourist trade from the US with thousands of people expected to fly across the Atlantic for an early summer break in London to enjoy the royal celebrations. Companies set up Jubilee tours while others offered royal themed holidays outside of the central weekend that included visits to a string of regal settings. Tourist attractions added their own Jubilee elements in the months running up to the celebrations.

The Royal Family is estimated to bring in around £550 million in tourist trade every year, outside of the pandemic, with estimates that 2012 saw that go up to well over £1 billion. The true value of a Jubilee is hard to pin down – the figures in 2012 also included people visiting for the London Olympics. However, online booking sites for hotels and flights were all reporting increased demand for trips to London around the time of the Platinum Jubilee celebrations.

For those following from afar, the Platinum Jubilee was held in traditional style with plenty of images of flag waving crowds and smiling royals. An awareness of the historic significance of Elizabeth II's Platinum Jubilee led to worldwide interest, but concerns over her health in the run up to both the anniversary of her accession and the long weekend of festivities, as well as controversy over Commonwealth tours increased the global focus. The royal Jubilee of Elizabeth II had become a global phenomenon for a variety of reasons but, ultimately, that focus secured an international legacy for her, if not her dynasty.

## Chapter Nine

# Street Parties, Souvenirs and Celebrations

In the spring of 1810, as the fiftieth year of George III's reign passed its halfway mark, an obelisk was erected on the spot where a great feast had been held to mark the King's anniversary just months earlier. It was a fairly basic artwork with a simple, engraved plaque on the plinth that held it up but it had a special place in royal history for it became one of the first memorials of a British Royal Jubilee.

The obelisk was given by the 'Bachelors of Windsor' to their King for the 'particular esteem he has on all occasions manifested for their native town'. They took care to ensure that the details of the great ox roast that had marked the Jubilee on that spot in October 1809 were also mentioned. The King was too ill to unveil the monument but instead, Queen Charlotte turned up to do the royal honours and so began another Jubilee tradition. In the two centuries since, her descendants have unveiled thousands of commemorations for Jubilees with the mementoes forming a lasting legacy of these very royal celebrations.

Over 200 years after the 'Bachelors of Windsor' built an obelisk in honour of George III, a statue marking the Diamond Jubilee of Elizabeth II appeared nearby. 'The Windsor Lady' is also nestled in the area known as Bachelor's Acre. It shows the Queen with six of her favourite dogs, corgis, and was created in 2012 by Lydia Karpinska to mark the royal anniversary. That year, artwork of all types and sizes was unveiled across the UK to mark the Diamond Jubilee. Statues proved particularly popular, as they had at previous royal celebrations.

When Queen Victoria celebrated her Golden Jubilee, one of the first attempts to commemorate it came from a group of women who offered to raise funds to provide a gift chosen by their Monarch. Victoria, true to form, asked for a statue of Prince Albert. A sizeable chunk of the £90,000 they raised went towards a rendering of Albert but, as in the Jubilee of George III, it was decided charity should come first and a nursing institute to care for the poor in their own homes was established with the bulk of their fundraising efforts.

However, the desire to commemorate the Jubilee in sculpture had taken hold. Grand effigies of the Queen sprang up at the most symbolic seats of her power. In Windsor, a bronze statue of her by Sir Edgar Boehm was placed in the middle of the High Street, dominating the area. Victoria herself attended the official unveiling on 22 June 1887, sitting in a carriage nearby throughout the ceremony, despite her initial reluctance to have anything to do with her Jubilee. The streets were decked with flags and decorations and a large crowd gathered to see the statue revealed. Ten years later, the commemoration became a focal point in her Diamond Jubilee with the Queen once again visiting for an event marking her anniversary.

Victoria's journal entry for her Golden Jubilee Day, 20 June 1887, sees her note that despite a family around her, she felt 'quite alone' and the solitary nature of her sovereignty was underlined in another statue produced to mark the fiftieth anniversary of her reign. A marble version of Victoria was commissioned to stand outside Kensington Palace, where she had been born and educated and where she discovered she was Monarch. The statue shows her at the start of her reign, as the teenage queen of her Coronation, a reminder that she had begun her rule alone despite the all consuming influence of Prince Albert for part of her reign. It was designed by their daughter, Princess Louise, and selected in the year of the Golden Jubilee although it wasn't unveiled until 1893.

The Jubilee also saw smaller renderings of the Queen distributed across her realms. Francis John Williamson, a favourite artist of Queen

Victoria's, created a bust of the Sovereign which was reproduced and sent around country and Empire. This interpretation of Victoria, younger and slimmer than the Jubilee Queen herself and decked in the most symbolic gems in her collection, became a reminder of royal power to mark this very regal event.

Over 120 years later, at Elizabeth II's Diamond celebrations, this Jubilee practice was exercised once again at a more local level. Lancashire County Council commissioned a bronze bust of the Queen by local sculptor, Peter Hodgkinson, to be placed alongside a similar statue of Victoria, ordered in 1897 for her Diamond Jubilee. Twelve identical busts of Elizabeth II were also sent to each of Lancashire's twelve districts, spreading the image of the Queen at a vital moment in her reign far wider. The Queen and the Duke of Edinburgh also found themselves mirroring Victoria and Albert in another way in 2012. Statues of the two were created by Nina Bilbey, to stand at Canterbury Cathedral, close to similar renderings of the first Diamond Jubilee queen and her consort.

The original concept of a Jubilee paying for itself continued with many of the tributes of 2012 funded by local appeals. In Winchester, a bronze sculpture which showed an image of Elizabeth II inside a Hampshire rose was commissioned by the Lord Lieutenant, Dame Mary Fagan, and paid for by public donations. Residents of Windsor clubbed together to pay for one of the more unusual Diamond Jubilee sculptures. Lifesize replicas of two horses used to pull the carriage that the Queen travelled in for her celebrations were unveiled on the Long Walk as a memorial to the sixtieth anniversary of her reign.

George V had been less keen on statues to mark his Jubilee. One of the main memorials to his celebrations is the rather gloomy grey arch that stands on a stretch of the Thames renamed 'King's Reach' in 1935 as he marked twenty-five years on the throne. It features cherubs and a sea god, a nod to George's passion for the sea and the navy, but no rendering of the Monarch himself. However, George did put aside his preference for 'man of the people gestures' to pose for a dramatic portrait to mark his Silver Jubilee. Painted by John Lander, it depicts the Monarch in his Garter robes and places him in a classical and timeless setting, by a single column, with a focus firmly on the King at his Jubilee.

Victoria had been less keen to pose for portraits for her Jubilees. Dozens of unofficial portraits were created for her golden celebrations. One of Victoria's formal commissions was a painting of her extended family by Laurits Tuxen which depicted her with her many descendants and which she had been determined to create since her great rival in the European royal marriage stakes, the King of Denmark, had been painted with his many relations some years earlier. Victoria sits in the centre of the painting with a bust of Albert overlooking the whole scene, set in the Green Drawing Room of Windsor Castle.

It was a reminder that this Jubilee was all about Victoria and her dynasty as was another famous artwork from 1887. William Lockhart painted a romanticised image of the queen and her family during the Service of Thanksgiving at Westminster Abbey which went on to become one of the most famous images of Victoria's reign. A similar, soft focus rendering was painted by Frank Salisbury of the service for the Silver Jubilee of King George V. Both portraits feature sunbeams lighting the ancient church walls as a sign of divine blessing at a moment of royal celebration.

Victoria had preferred the more modern art form of photography for the pictorial souvenirs of her Jubilees with several of the photos she posed for becoming iconic images of her reign. Her decision, in 1897, to release one photo of her without copyright allowed it to be reproduced around the Empire with ease and ensured the image she wanted for herself and her Monarchy became the dominant one. The paintings marking her Diamond Jubilee again centred on the celebrations, with a well known depiction by Gennaro d'Amato, showing the Queen at St. Paul's Cathedral for the service marking that anniversary.

As a result, the lasting public souvenirs of Britain's royal jubilees have become the large scale artworks like the Victoria statues that take centre stage in famous locations. Elizabeth II, too, has been portrayed in relatively few paintings for her Jubilees. The only official painted portrait of the Queen for her sixtieth anniversary was the work of Ralph Heimans. Entitled 'The Coronation Theatre', it showed Elizabeth II in her Robe of State in an empty abbey, her head bowed in contemplation.

The historic significance of Jubilee memorials was shown in the keen interest in acquiring this portrait. It was originally on show at the National Portrait Gallery of Australia throughout 2012 where it attracted a record number of visitors. It was then displayed at Westminster Abbey in a special exhibition in 2013 marking sixty years since the Coronation. A private donation allowed the Abbey to buy it for its new Diamond Jubilee Galleries which were created in a thirteenth-century part of the ancient church which had never been opened to the public before. There, the Abbey's long association with the British Monarchy is on show for all to see with Elizabeth II's historic painting sitting among manuscripts highlighting royal power.

The creation of the Diamond Jubilee Galleries is characteristic of another trait of anniversary celebrations. Since the very first royal Jubilee in Britain, these unique public events have been marked by bestowing their rather unusual name on anything and everything. In 1897, the Diamond Jubilee Sunset Home for Aged People opened its doors in London, while the Diamond Jubilee Nursing Association also began its mission in Burnham-on-Sea in Somerset that year. Newmarket in Suffolk became home to one of hundreds of clocks put up to mark the Diamond Jubilee. In 1887, the Queen Victoria Jubilee Institute for Nurses made its debut.

The desire to attach the world 'Jubilee' to buildings to mark the event led to the UK Cabinet Office issuing guidance for people hoping to celebrate the Queen's seventy-year reign by naming a place to mark the event. The rules stated that the use of 'Jubilee' or 'Platinum

Jubilee' was fine for re-naming but that anything more regal, such as Queen Elizabeth II's Platinum Jubilee, needed to be checked by a special team. They also revealed that they expected applications to come to them throughout 2022 with many people anticipated to make their tribute after the main Jubilee weekend.

They would join a sizeable group of streets, roads and squares whose names were inspired by these royal anniversaries. As 2022 got under way there were already over 600 thoroughfares named 'Jubilee' across the UK. The most popular name is 'Jubilee Road' with over 120 examples followed by 'Jubilee Close' with more than 100 existing in the UK. Jubilee Avenue, Jubilee Way and Jubilee Street are also popular as is Jubilee Gardens. Peterborough and Birmingham postcodes are the most common among the streets called Jubilee.

A handful of places have more specific names with at least four examples of Golden Jubilee Way found and three versions of Diamond Jubilee Way existing. Meanwhile, the Office of National Statistics data shows that the stars of Jubilees continue to have an impact on place names. Queen Street remains the twenty-third most popular road name in England while Victoria Street is at twenty-four and King Street at twenty-five. George Street makes it to number thirty. Most towns and cities in England have at least one residence named 'Jubilee House' or 'Jubilee Villa', carved into the white stone panels above the main door.

It's not just places that have been named after Jubilees. The popular interest in the very first royal celebration, for George III, led to a strange baby craze that has continued ever since. Baptismal records across England show that a number of the babies born on the first British Jubilee Day, 25 October 1809, ended up with the word as a very personal souvenir in the form of one of their names. Jubilee Mary Leicester was born in Ashton-under-Lyne while in Richmond, Surrey, the Gillmore family welcomed Jubilee Elizabeth. In Liverpool, George Jubilee Howood made his debut while hundreds of miles away, in Wiltshire, George Jubilee Chapman also found himself named in honour of both king and royal celebration.

Between October and December 1809, around 500 birth entries for babies who were given Jubilee as either a first or middle name are found in remaining records. By 1881, just before the next Jubilee, the Census for England and Wales has several hundred entries for 'Jubilees' born around 1809 with an even split between men and women.

Queen Victoria's celebrations in 1887 caused another surge of Jubilee babies. Interest in the name grew in the months before her celebrations, with usage rising from an average of two babies a year to thirty registrations in one quarter. By the time the Golden Jubilee arrived, that number had risen again with around 250 babies given Jubilee as a first name as the celebrations took place. In 1897, some parents went even further as Diamond Jubilee Reckless, born in Rotherham, and Diamond Jubilee Price from Putney could both attest. The 1911 Census for England shows nine teenagers called Diamond Jubilee, born in the year of Victoria's celebration, including a thirteen year old whose surname did him no favours, leaving him to go through life as Edward Diamond Jubilee Day.

The patriotic resonance that led to the name Jubilee taking hold would also lead to poignancy. The Commonwealth War Graves Register of 1917 includes an entry for 12 March noting the death of Acting Leading Stoker Jubilee John Brashier, killed when the submarine he was serving on was mined off the Shetlands. He was thirty, born at the time of Queen Victoria's Golden Jubilee in 1887. Private Jubilee John Whatling, born in the year of Victoria's Diamond anniversary, was killed on 19 April 1918 in the last months of the First World War. In 1941, Petty Officer Jubilee Jack Tweed, aged forty-four, died when HMS *Mashona* sank after being attacked by German bombers. Others with Jubilee as a middle name were claimed in both conflicts, all killed fighting for the country whose national celebration had helped name them.

The celebrations for King George V didn't have quite the same impact on first name picks. A polite smattering of 'Jubilees' are found in birth records for the second quarter of 1935 when George marked his anniversary and after that, the use becomes almost obsolete. The Jubilees of Elizabeth II have seen even less interest in the name and, when used, confined to girls. However, the names of members of the Royal Family grew in popularity during the Diamond Jubilee with Harry becoming the most used boy's name of the year and Elizabeth surging once more. The impact of royalty on everyday life was still being felt.

The Jubilee name trend has never been adopted by the Royal Family themselves. Queen Victoria welcomed a granddaughter in 1887, just months after her golden celebrations. The baby was described by her father as the 'little Jubilee grandchild' but christened Victoria Eugenie Julia Ena instead. In 1935, King George V welcomed a grandson who was christened Edward with no hint of Jubilee in his middle names. The Queen became a grandmother for the first time in the year of her Silver Jubilee but her Jubilee grandchild was called Peter Mark Andrew.

However, later Jubilees continue to inspire a change of names for parts of the world. The expected spate of namings for Platinum Jubilee year began within hours of 2022 getting under way. The Australian government made the first big commemorative announcement with confirmation that Aspen Island in Canberra's Lake Burley Griffin would become Queen Elizabeth II Island to mark seventy years of royal rule. The decision to create a natural space to commemorate this Jubilee would be a popular theme in 2022.

The environment became a major area for celebrations in the Platinum Jubilee as the Royal Family continued to make it one of its major focuses. The Queen's Green Canopy was designed as a lasting legacy of the celebrations for seventy years of Elizabeth II's rule. People across the Commonwealth were urged to 'plant a tree for the Jubilee'. The Queen got the event under way, rooting a tree on the Balmoral Estate with the help of Prince Charles at the very start of October 2021, the beginning of planting season. In the months that followed, members of the Royal Family helped build the canopy with plantings around the world. The scheme also aimed to identify seventy ancient trees across Britain to mark the Queen's seven decades of service. Seventy ancient woodlands around the UK were also dedicated for the Jubilee.

The Woodland Trust donated thousands of free saplings to community organisations across the UK as part of the scheme. Ten years earlier, the organisation had helped oversee another green project to mark the Diamond celebrations of Elizabeth II when it had organised the Jubilee Woods project which aimed to plant six million trees across the UK as a legacy. In both instances, the Trust took on the role of liaising with landowners and organisations to find suitable space to create the projects.

The call to plant trees for the Jubilee echoed the sentiments of previous Jubilees. In Hungerford, the organisers of local celebrations found themselves with money left over after marking the Golden Jubilee of Queen Victoria and so used the surplus to reinvigorate an area of local trees. It tapped into one of the dominant themes of the very first royal celebrations of 1809 when initial opposition to the idea of a massive royal party had led to calls for the anniversary to be marked with philanthropy and events that would help others on a long term basis.

That same desire to turn the Jubilee into a charitable event for George III would leave another legacy. The first celebrations had begun with proposals for huge feasts that had been expanded further by popular pressure. Alongside the great gala dinners, there were to be publicly funded meals for the poor. The roast beef and plum pudding of 1809 had been served to those in need in their own homes or at huge tables where they joined others in the community for a celebratory meal. The sharing of food to mark Jubilees has become one of its most emblematic moments, with feasting present at all British celebrations.

The anniversary of George III saw hundreds of communal meals to mark Jubilee Day itself. The Royal Family, led by Queen Charlotte in lieu of her ailing husband, headed to Bachelor's Wood to join in the ox roast that would later lead to that first Jubilee monument. Around Britain, similar ox roasts were held with the people of Chester following their dinner as it made its final walk through the city in procession with the butcher about to prepare it.

Subscriptions and fundraisers had led to the provision of luxurious meals for the poor as well as for prisoners and debtors who all feasted like royalty, if only for one day. Meanwhile, the great and the good paid handsomely for spectacular dinners that became the ticket everyone wanted to get their hands on. That combination of public partying and gala evenings would be followed through subsequent Jubilees.

Just as at the time of George III's Jubilee, ox roasts were held for Victoria's golden celebrations with the people of Skipton following the tradition of parading their meal through the streets, this time decked in a union flag ready for the photographers, before the butcher got to work. In 1897, commemorative plates were issued in Leeds to those who attended the Jubilee roast there.

The *West Herts Post* of 1887 noted that a local farmer had offered the use of a field near to Croxley Green for the Jubilee feast. Other generous residents donated beef and beer while many contributed to the fund to pay for the celebrations. The Jubilee day also included sports, games and a best dressed baby contest as people took advantage of time off work to celebrate. Victoria's sixtieth anniversary saw the people of Matlock in Derbyshire put on a special dinner for all those aged sixty or more, attended by over 200 hungry participants. Schools put on teas for all pupils with over 1,200 children joining in. Meanwhile, a local landowner handed over one of his fields for the day to allow sports and games to be played to mark the event.

The 1887 celebrations had also seen Queen Victoria attend the 'Children's Jubilee' at Hyde Park where 30,000 youngsters had been entertained to tea and cake in huge tents before being given the run of the green spaces and a wide range of entertainment laid on for them, including puppet shows, performing animals and lucky dips. Military bands played while the Queen observed it all from a discreet distance with a handful of well behaved children invited to present her with flowers. This focus on putting on parties for children would be echoed in later Jubilees.

By the Silver Jubilee of George V, the local feasts which had been part of celebrations since 1809 began to take on a different design and young people were at the heart of that. The end of the First World War had led to a call for 'peace teas' where individual streets or groups of streets held parties, primarily for children who had been orphaned in the war. They were organised around Peace Day which was earmarked for 19 July 1919, following the signing of the Treaty of Versailles. Elements of communal celebrations enjoyed during Victoria's Jubilees, including bunting and street decorations, were organised on a small scale level while party tables were laid with sandwiches, cakes and treats. The street party had been born.

By the time of George V's Jubilee, the idea had gained currency and street parties were held across Britain. Rather than local councils looking for subscriptions to provide large scale meals for the poor, the new way of celebration involved small groups of people putting together a party outside their front door. Long tables down the middle of the street were laid with party food, all made by residents or picked up from the corner shop. Children were the main focus of the street party but as the al fresco idea continued to evolve, they embraced all age groups.

In 1977 they had become one of the main focuses of celebrating the Queen's Silver Jubilee. Over 10 million people attended a street party for that royal anniversary. In one part of West Ham, bunting and flags were strung between windows on opposite sides of the street while children in fancy dress settled down to a party tea. Later, the same tables were laid with drinks and crisps for their older relatives to have their own celebrations. These street parties were often homemade through and through. Families pooled resources, with dining tables carried out of front parlours and laid end to end with borrowed chairs lined up on either side. Record players were placed at open windows to provide music while food poured out of kitchens and into the streets. One of the iconic sights of 1977 was streets across Britain, decked in red, white and blue and filled with people wearing handmade crowns.

By the later Jubilees of Elizabeth II, the street party had become so integral to the celebrations that local councils, who gave permission for roads to be closed for the events, often started preparations for the deluge of applications several years before the royal anniversaries approached. By the time of the Platinum Jubilee, the UK government had set up a website where people could check the requirements of their local authority and link through to online applications with their council.

There were also attempts to formalise the street party. While thousands still took place in the new Elizabethan tradition of local residents coming together, thousands more took part in the Big Jubilee Lunch which was first launched in 2012 and became a central plank of the 2022 celebrations, too. The Big Lunch scheme was launched in 2009 and aimed to bring people across local communities together on a designated day in summer, to share food and company. It was designed to bolster links between all age groups in local areas. It was also built on a different scale to the street party. While whole roads could get involved, the Big Lunch also called for people to try to come together in any setting, even if it was just a few friends in a back garden.

For the Diamond and Platinum Jubilees of Elizabeth II, the Big Lunch became a part of the celebrations. The initial announcements for the special weekend marking the seventieth anniversary of the Queen's reign included the Big Lunch in the line up. The final day of that weekend, 5 June, was earmarked in particular for celebrations but the special online resources suggested any time across the four day party was appropriate. The Jubilee celebrations also formed part of a special month dedicated to supporting local communities. Two hundred years after the idea was first suggested, ensuring Jubilees put royalty at the heart of celebrations across the nation remained integral.

Street parties had also become big business. One of the first souvenirs to hit the shops in the twenty-first century Jubilees were paper plates and cups, designed for these communal celebrations. Meanwhile, a competition to find a pudding fit for the Queen was also launched. The Platinum Pudding contest aimed to create a dessert that millions across Britain would serve up at their street party. The Royal Family would be expected to taste and celebrate it and perhaps even serve it at any banquets they held to mark the event. Since the first Jubilee, glittering parties for the royal anniversary had formed part of all celebrations. In 1809, Queen Charlotte had hosted the most talked about Jubilee party in the grounds of her favourite residence, Frogmore House at Windsor. Almost eighty years later, Charlotte's granddaughter, Queen Victoria, began the fiftieth anniversary of her reign with a meal outside at Frogmore. However, Victoria invited her closest relations to a breakfast near to the mausoleum where her beloved husband, Albert, was buried.

Later that evening, she was joined by dozens of royals, most of them related to her, for a banquet held at Buckingham Palace to mark her Jubilee. The kings of the Belgians, of Denmark and of the Hellenes joined the Crown Prince of Portugal and the heir to the throne of Norway and Sweden around a table loaded with three soups, three fish dishes and a trio of entrees as well as roast beef and haunch of venison, chicken and an array of cold meats and vegetables. But the pretty menu card, decorated with golden swirls containing the floral symbols of England, Scotland, Wales and Ireland made no mention of 'Jubilee'. Instead, this was, simply, 'Her Majesty's Dinner', a nod to Victoria's sometimes wary attitude towards marking the anniversary.

King George V marked his Silver Jubilee with a ball for several thousand people at Buckingham Palace while his granddaughter, Elizabeth II, used several of her Jubilees to gather the crowned heads of other nations for a lunch and group photos which served as pictorial histories of their own. The modern House of Windsor has tended to shy away from ostentatious balls and gala dinners, putting the focus on popular celebrations instead.

The twenty-first century anniversaries have also seen a huge growth in the Jubilee souvenir market. The Royal Collection Trust, which looks after many royal treasures, launched official Platinum souvenirs in 2021 with a secondary collection appearing in March 2022, three months before the big celebratory weekend. The actual seventieth anniversary of the Queen's reign, in February 2022, saw a rush of commemorative mugs, plates and tea towels hit the shops while online portals like etsy and eBay were flooded with souvenirs, from badges to banners.

Marking Jubilees with trinkets like teapots or sweet dishes made money for Victorian entrepreneurs as well. From the late nineteenth century onwards, royal events became popular for souvenir sellers with Victoria's fiftieth anniversary as queen becoming a golden opportunity. Plates and cups were particularly popular items for mass production. One of the earliest to go on sale to mark the fiftieth year of her reign as a whole, with its elaborate decoration giving the date of 21 June 1886 was released at the beginning of Victoria's Golden Jubilee year. The plates were often given fancy shapes with one octagonal design showing her as a young queen and as the empress of 1887 with pictorial representations of several of the realms she ruled.

Jubilee cups went into mass production for the first time for Victoria's Golden Jubilee with local versions produced as mementoes for school children or as relatively cheap souvenirs of this big royal event. The Scarborough edition, made by Doulton, featured an elaborate sepia-toned image as well as the date of the Jubilee celebrations and Victoria's name. China beakers were particularly popular with many produced in plain white with a simple decoration reminding its user of the Queen's dates and glorious titles. Glassware also made it into the shops with double-sided dishes, each half bearing one of the dates of Victoria's reign, a popular design. More unusual items included an intricately carved glass perfume bottle with a rendering of Victoria's face on its front. As Jubilee day approached, the royal image and story appeared on everything from biscuit tins to brass plaques as royalty made the tills ring.

By 1897 the souvenir industry had expanded further. The focus on empire during these celebrations was reflected in decorations on commemorative china and glassware. Mugs were more elaborate and production techniques saw many more manufactured in colour rather than the monochrome which dominated Golden Jubilee souvenirs. The designs were more involved, too, with one beaker scrolled with the patriotic verse 'the pillar of a people's hope, the centre of a world's desire' and several mass produced drawings of Victoria at various stages of her life. Enamel beakers were another popular choice for commemorative merchandise while the standard plates of the past Jubilee were joined by a number of tea sets. Pottery was also mass produced for this celebration and nearly every design to hit the shops featured a similar rendering of Victoria, empress-like with her crown and veil. The Queen who had retreated behind a curtain of grief for part of her reign was now ever present, her image imported into millions of homes in the form of cheap souvenirs for her Jubilee.

The role of gifts and trinkets as a way of boosting royal image could be seen in the small items that could be quickly and easily distributed en masse, placing the queen at the heart of yet more families. In Bradford-on-Avon, new public baths were opened in the year of Queen Victoria's Diamond Jubilee with commemorative medals struck for the occasion. On one side was a rendering of the Monarch herself, becoming a royal presence in homes around the area for years to come.

By the Silver Jubilee of King George V, the royal image was being shared on even more useful items that might see a Monarch pass through a household's hands several times in a day. Commemorative spoons were popular in 1935 while tea tins bearing pictures of George and his wife, Queen Mary, also hit the shops. Beakers and mugs remained constant commemorative tools, but this Jubilee also saw wider circulation of celebratory magazines and inexpensive books to mark the occasion. The rise of photography meant that the badges that had become so popular as souvenirs for past Jubilees could now bear a truly lifelike image of the King and his consort.

The Silver Jubilee of his granddaughter, Elizabeth II, in 1977, saw photos dominate the souvenirs on sale. The traditional chinaware of Jubilees was now stamped with photographic images of the Monarch as were the tea towels that would become a staple souvenir of the Elizabethan celebrations. Books, including special Ladybird editions for children, were mass produced while souvenirs became even more imaginative with socks, t-shirts and shopping bags joining the line up. It was a pattern repeated at the Golden and Diamond Jubilees. By the time the Queen marked her Platinum Jubilee, souvenirs had already been on sale for months.

As Elizabeth II's reign reached its seventieth anniversary, the Royal Collection Trust had already been selling official Jubilee mugs and tea towels for several months and released a new range, featuring the official emblem of the celebrations, soon afterwards. Meanwhile, private companies were releasing their own merchandise before 2022 got under way with an eye, too, on the international market. The Jubilees of the twenty-first century had become global affairs and websites selling royal linked souvenirs were ready to ship around the world as interest in this royal anniversary went far beyond the boundaries of Elizabeth II's realms.

Across the Commonwealth, another Jubilee tradition was observed in 2022. Since Victoria's golden celebrations, official Jubilee medals had been produced and distributed to select groups. In 1887, a

Golden Jubilee medal had been struck for those involved with the celebrations and for the military. Members of the Royal Family and the Royal Household as well as government officials were presented with it as were specially chosen army and navy officers. It was also presented to envoys and ambassadors as well as leading politicians from around the Empire. The medal featured an engraving of a bust of Victoria by Joseph Boehm on one side with a wreath on the other around the words 'in commemoration of the fiftieth year of the reign of Queen Victoria, 21 June 1887'. It wasn't quite as egalitarian as it sounded, though, for different versions of the medal were made with the golden creations handed out to Victoria's family. Others received silver or bronze versions.

A Diamond Jubilee decoration followed in 1897 although those who had already been awarded a medal in 1887 received a bar instead, reading 1897, to attach to their existing ribbon. The later medal bore the same design but was also struck in a diamond shape to be presented to mayors and provosts across Britain, again with a superior gold version for those who bore the dignity of lord mayor or provost. The Diamond Jubilee also saw the creation of a special medal for police officers on duty during the celebrations.

By the time of King George V's Jubilee, the medal had become a highly important element of the celebrations for the Royal Household. In 1935, over 85,000 medals were awarded across the Empire with the new air force included for the first time along with local government officials. George's Jubilee medal showed him with Queen Mary who is also mentioned in the inscription. The other side bore the initials 'GRI', a reminder that George was the first British royal to see his official rule as Emperor reach a Jubilee – Victoria hadn't assumed that title until 1876 and so never marked a major anniversary as an Empress.

Her great, great granddaughter, Elizabeth II, was Head of the Commonwealth rather than an imperial ruler by the time her own Silver Jubilee arrived. In 1977, David Wynne produced a modern design featuring the Queen wearing a rather large crown with another crown on the other side of the medal. A different design was used in Canada as it was in 2002. The Golden Jubilee medal of Elizabeth II was produced with a gilt finish, making it the first to be distributed widely in a golden design rather than silver. By 2002, prison officers were also included in the list of those eligible for the medal. Like the members of the emergency services and military who received it, they had to have at least five years service completed by the time the Queen reached the fiftieth anniversary of her accession. The same rules governed the Diamond Jubilee medal which featured a diamond shape on one side, containing the Queen's dates.

Its designer, Timothy Noad, was called upon to create the Platinum Jubilee medal which was revealed in October 2021. Featuring a portrait of the Queen on one side and the royal crest with the dates of Elizabeth II's reign on the other, its motto reverted to tradition. The words around the image read 'Elizabeth II Dei Gratia Regina Fid Def' (Elizabeth II, By the Grace of God, Queen, Defender of the Faith).

The design was widely praised but the potential distribution of the medal ran into controversy. As it was revealed, the Duke of York found himself embroiled in a civil court case in the United States. There was public debate about whether Prince Andrew, who eventually settled out of court, should be given the medal which would be distributed to all members of the Royal Family. Much more popular was the decision to present it to all living recipients of the Victoria and George Crosses as well as frontline emergency workers and military with five years or more service.

Along with medals, special coins had become a staple of Jubilee souvenirs. In 2022, the Royal Mint issued its first ever 50p commemorating a major royal event with the special design, personally approved by the Queen, entering circulation on 7 February 2022, the day after her reign reached seventy years. The number 70 features prominently in the design with the Queen's royal cypher inside the zero and her dates underneath that. Collector's editions had already been released following a pattern set at previous jubilees. In 2012, a commemorative £5 coin featuring images of Elizabeth II at the start of her reign and at the time of her Diamond Jubilee was released by the Royal Mint, on sale for just a year. Its value was a reference to the traditional use of a crown for commemorative editions – a special version of that coin had gone on sale in 1977 to mark the Silver Jubilee.

The Platinum Jubilee stamps entered circulation on the same day as the special 50p with a series of eight designs on sale at Post Offices as soon as Elizabeth II had completed seven decades as Queen. The set followed a pattern begun in 2012 when a series of images, including pictures from the Silver and Golden Jubilees, were chosen for the commemorative edition marking the Diamond celebrations. A set released earlier in 2012 showed Elizabeth II alongside the other Monarchs of the House of Windsor as another Jubilee tribute.

Stamps had first been associated with Jubilees as far back as Victoria's reign although then it had been more about marketing than marking the Monarchy. A new set was released on 1 January 1887 and quickly became known as the Jubilee set although they had been planned for several years. At the time, commemorative stamps weren't issued but the popularity of the design and the decision to release them as Jubilee year got under way ended up associating them with the celebrations ever afterwards. They became known as the Jubilee stamps and included the first ever two-tone British stamps. Their innovative design and royal links meant they stayed on sale until the end of Victoria's reign.

King George V was a noted philatelist with one of the most admired stamp collections of the time but it was the Colonial Office which suggested a commemorative set for his Silver Jubilee which it hoped would be issued across the Empire. Planning began in 1934 with artists invited to submit ideas but none of the early offerings won royal favour. Instead, George ended up selecting a design by Barnett Freedman which went on sale on 7 May 1935, three days before the Jubilee. The large, landscape style stamp featured the king's head with the legend 'Silver Jubilee' above it and the dates of his reign on either side of his profile.

The Silver Jubilee stamps of his granddaughter, Elizabeth II, made a reference to that design. Issued by the Royal Mail on 11 May 1977, they again took a large, landscape shape with the Queen's head at the centre. The letters 'E' and 'R' stood on either side of her profile while, just as with George V's stamps, the words Silver Jubilee were written across the top. The dates of her reign at the time sat at the bottom of the stamps and, just like those of 1935, different colours were used for different values. The stamps were also sold as first day covers with postmarks covering individual stops on the Queen's Silver Jubilee tour, a marketing tool on show for the first time.

Promoting the royal image had been at the heart of the very first British royal jubilee and the explosion of permanent commemorations for these anniversaries only carries that idea further. Charlotte Biggs' decision to remind Britain of just how important their king was to them as she devised George III's Golden Jubilee has been echoed in the way that the royal image and the royal name have been stamped around the country during Jubilees.

However, permanent mementoes weren't high on the priority list for that first Jubilee. The obelisk at Bachelor's Wood came several months after the celebrations. Thomas Preston, who wrote about the Jubilee decades later as Victoria's golden anniversary approached, noted that many houses across the land might find in a drawer an old blue ribbon. Without knowing it, many people had kept a record of the Georgian Jubilee. On 25 October 1809, many of his wealthier subjects had worn a dark blue ribbon with his likeness attached or simply the words of his name. Poorer relations might have run to a more tattered ribbon in regal blue. Preston noted that many of these had been tucked away and their significance forgotten, but those pieces of material, hidden from view, had become the first examples of what would become one of the most important ways of distributing the royal image – jubilee souvenirs.

# Chapter Ten

# Jubilee and Image, Being Seen to be Believed

Among the many famous quotes from her reign, the Queen's observation on the power of image remains one of the best known. '*I have to be seen to be believed*', runs the line and Jubilees have always provided the Monarchy with an opportunity to be seen but the beliefs that spring from that can be as challenging as they are triumphant.

The Queen herself experienced that first hand as her Platinum Jubilee celebrations took shape in 2022. The main events were announced a year in advance with the official emblem appearing soon afterwards to put a kind of royal corporate stamp across coverage. Official souvenirs followed along with confirmation of the first Jubilee tours. There was also very public royal support for Jubilee schemes to reward volunteers and bring communities together through Big Lunches after the pandemic. The Monarchy was making itself very visible indeed and in the most positive way, but the more it was seen, the more those beliefs in it were challenged.

The House of Windsor has always excited huge media interest but as Elizabeth II became the only British Monarch to rule for seventy years, the focus on her family intensified. The forthcoming celebrations seemed to give parts of the media an opportunity to run a negative story and then run it again with the word 'Jubilee' in the headline. In the early weeks of 2022, when Buckingham Palace issued a statement saying that the Duke of York had handed back all his patronages and military associations at a time when he was settling a civil case over allegations of sexual assault, the timing allowed it to run time and time again with a Jubilee angle.

After the Duke of York walked his mother into the memorial service for his father, just ten weeks before the long weekend of celebrations, papers were again filled with headlines asking if Andrew would now be at the Jubilee. As the Duke of Sussex took a court case against the Home Office over security arrangements, the same question was asked about Harry and whether his worries might stop him standing at his grandmother's side for her historic celebrations. Meanwhile, the first of the Platinum Jubilee tours was pulled apart by critics who claimed the Duke and Duchess of Cambridge's time in the Caribbean reeked of colonialism and showed a Monarchy out of touch with modern life.

It was far from a fairy tale start to the celebrations but the majority of British Royal Jubilees have taken shape when the royal family sees its image waning. Only the Diamond celebrations of Victoria and Elizabeth II developed with the Monarchy on the up. The very idea of a Jubilee had been born when ardent royalists became concerned that sentiment against the throne was so strong that it might end up toppling it. The Silver Jubilees of George V and his granddaughter fell in years when unemployment was rising and people's incomes were shrinking, while the Golden Jubilee of Elizabeth II unfolded just a few years after loud calls for the Crown to topple after the death of Diana, Princess of Wales. And yet every single celebration has ended with a show of support that has catapulted it into success.

One reason is the consistency of the message sent out at these royal celebrations. Well worn devices to spread the positive image of the throne have been used time and again and have underlined the deep roots that royalty has in British life. Official emblems are relatively new, first introduced for the Silver celebrations of 1977 but by 2022 they had become an integral part of the events. The Platinum Jubilee logo, designed by student Edward Roberts, was released without any restrictions on its use, allowing anyone to use it and making it an easy option for all those seeking Jubilee branding. By the spring of 2022, it was a regular sight and even made it on to souvenir socks.

It was based around that most potent of royal images, the crown, but this ultimate symbol of royal power has had a limited role to play in Jubilee celebrations. Ever since Queen Victoria refused to wear her crown for the Service of Thanksgiving for her Golden Jubilee, royal regalia has been relegated to a back seat in the imagery of the Jubilee.

The Queen did pose for an official portrait for her Silver Jubilee wearing her Robe of State and the Imperial State Crown but the photo, by Peter Gurgeon, was overlooked as an image of the celebrations in favour of the pictures of Elizabeth II, dressed in pink, on the main day of celebrations. Her Diamond Jubilee saw the Queen photographed again in her Robe of State but this time wearing the George IV Diadem and Coronation necklace. The image, by John Swannell, again took second place in the iconography of the day to the photos of Elizabeth II wearing diamond white and sailing down the Thames amidst thousands of little boats during the Jubilee regatta.

The crown, in an almost oversized rendering, dominates the Silver Jubilee medal of Elizabeth II. The image, by David Wynne, was placed on the tens of thousands of medals distributed in 1977 to those involved in the Jubilee celebrations. Over 30,000 were handed out in Britain with the same number distributed in Canada and thousands more presented elsewhere in the Commonwealth. The awarding of Jubilee medals has been a way of showing the Crown's gratitude since Victorian times and has become an important part of the imagery of these anniversary celebrations.

George III's Jubilee of 1809 had seen the production of several medals and medallions but they were unofficial in character. In 1887, a Golden Jubilee medal was commissioned to be presented to everyone involved in Victoria's celebrations. While the Royal Family were at the top of the recipients' list, the largesse spread much further. Members of the Royal Household, government officials as well as members of the colonial governments were all eligible. So, too, were members of the Armed Forces involved in Jubilee celebrations. The medal featured a bust of Victoria by Edgar Boehm who had modelled many of the Jubilee renderings of the Queen, thus ensuring the image of the Monarch at this high point of her reign remained consistent. He also had a say in the obverse, choosing Clemens Emptmayer to design a wreath which was placed around the word 'In commemoration of the 50th year of the reign of Queen Victoria, 21 June 1887'. It was to be worn on the left breast, before campaign medals.

In 1897 the process was repeated but refined and expanded. A gold version of the medal was given to members of the Royal Family while a silver was presented to officers who had taken part in the celebrations. The bronze version was reserved for other ranks who had taken part in the parade. Meanwhile, the mayors of Britain were all awarded a silver, diamond shaped medal bearing the Queen's image for the Jubilee with a gold version reserved for the Lord Mayors and Provosts of the country. Separate medals were issued for both occasions for the police. Over the course of the two Jubilees, over 25,000 medals went to officers across London with fire officers and ambulance staff included in the presentations for the Diamond celebrations.

By the time of George V's Jubilee the reach of the medal, designed by Sir William Goscombe John and featuring the King and his consort, Queen Mary, was much wider. Over 85,000 were produced with the government deciding how many should be sent to the King's dominions and how many would be awarded at home. By the time of the Silver Jubilee of Elizabeth II, Commonwealth countries could decide themselves how many medals were handed over. Throughout all Jubilees, the criteria for medals has remained the same with those involved in the celebrations in an official capacity being rewarded. In 2002, a pattern of recognising police and emergency service workers and military with five years or more service at the time of the anniversary was established. That medal was issued in cupronickel with a gilt finish as a nod to the name of the Jubilee and is the only one of the special awards to be presented to all recipients in that colour.

By 2012, many Commonwealth countries were issuing their own version of the medal and it became the most widely distributed of all Jubilee awards. Over 450,000 members of the Armed Forces were eligible, placing an image of royal recognition in households across the country. The impact of the medal was seen in complaints that some groups, including the Merchant Navy, had been left out. In 2022 the Platinum Jubilee design, by Timothy Noad, was awarded along the same lines with the RNLI added to the list of recipients.

The medals show appreciation in a very public way. The Monarchy was boosted among the officials receiving the medals through this act of gratitude. But the proud recipients also wore their awards back home, ensuring the ultimate royal image remained on show around the country for months and years to come, a constant reminder of the Jubilee itself. The image of the Monarch, at the height of their powers, became part of the everyday life of communities around their realm, a positive legacy of the celebrations.

Newspapers in 1897 bemoaned that in a Jubilee year, virtually everything found itself in some way associated with the celebrations. The issue for the royal celebrating the anniversary, certainly since Victoria's second Jubilee, is to make sure that the positive outweighs the negative. The very nature of Jubilees sees much of the celebrating initiated at personal and local levels as people organise street parties for a few neighbours or schools ask pupils to write stories or draw pictures to mark the occasion. For those involved, that becomes the abiding memory and some official celebrations fall into the background as a result.

For centuries, the Poet Laureate has marked major royal events with a special composition. However, their Jubilee efforts are never among the best known. Although lines are written, and sometimes read aloud, they are usually a somewhat overlooked part of the celebrations. In 1977, when the post was held by one of its most popular occupants, Sir John Betjeman, his many works to mark the Silver Jubilee all took second place to the massive interest in the Sex

Pistols single 'God Save The Queen' with its controversial lyrics and symbolic cover imagery that blanked out parts of the Monarch's face with the title of the song.

In 2012, as Britain boomed in a summer when everyone wanted to come to London, Carol Ann Duffy didn't just write for the celebrations in her role as Poet Laureate, she gathered in work by other artists to mark the anniversary. A compilation of sixty poems, one for each year of the Queen's reign, was produced with 'Jubilee Lines' also recorded for an online project. Some of the biggest TV stars of the time, including Downton Abbey's Dan Stevens, read the works which were accompanied by striking art work representing the sound waves that each composition made. However, it had to compete with spectacular events for coverage.

In 2002, official poetry was mixed with popular outreach in a competition for children to write their own memento of the Golden Jubilee. Over 4,000 entries were received and the fifty best, chosen by a panel including Poet Laureate Andrew Motion, were included in an anthology to mark the event. It was more successful that the official poetry created for Queen Victoria's Golden Jubilee. Her Poet Laureate, Alfred, Lord Tennyson's offering was widely ridiculed. It began with a reflection on the length of Victoria's reign that would lead to almost instant parody.

*'Fifty times the rose has flower'd and faded, fifty times the golden harvest fallen, since our Queen assumed the globe, the sceptre.'*

It added a hint of the ancient meaning of Jubilee, with its focus on remission and restoration, saying '*let the weary be comforted, let the needy be banqueted, let the maim'd in his heart rejoice, at this year of her Jubilee.'*

A journal, *The Weekly Dispatch*, held a competition for the best parody of Tennyson's much criticised memorial with prizes of two guineas. The entries included plenty of attacks on the Poet Laureate's style but also became an outlet for anti-Jubilee frustration. *'Fifty times the rose has flower'd and faded, fifty times it would have bloomed without her – smelt as sweet without the crown, the sceptre.'*

Another was yet more scathing: '*are there children starving in our alleys? Are there famine stricken homes in cities? Trust not Queen or Lords to feed the people...'* The official celebrations had opened the door for scathing criticisms.

More successful was the contribution of the Bishop of Wakefield to Queen Victoria's Diamond Jubilee. He wrote the words for a special hymn that was sung in all churches on the anniversary of her accession, 20 June 1897. It proved popular but Victoria and her advisers had chosen well with their author. William Walsham How was known as 'the poor man's bishop' and 'the children's bishop' for his work among some of the most deprived communities in England. His hymn was one of thanks to God for all the blessings of the time and ended with a prayer for help to continue on the path of goodness. It was a huge hit with the Jubilee Queen herself who wrote of it frequently in her journals as her special year came to an end.

Art around a Jubilee has had varying levels of success. The more regal official portraits are often less popular than the more informal poses. As she reached the seventieth anniversary of her reign, the Queen was photographed at her official red boxes with a picture of her father, George VI, at her side. It was an instant hit and, unlike 2012, it was the only official record of that momentous day. Ten years earlier, the rather regal portrait of Elizabeth II decked in diamonds and standing in front of the Victoria Memorial, had been shared on the anniversary of her accession. The less formal approach to an arguably bigger celebration was a striking development.

But the twenty-first century also brought a fuller awareness that all parts of a Jubilee were of huge interest to millions. Royal residences now put on exhibitions to mark the anniversaries with the display of diamonds at Buckingham Palace for the Queen's sixtieth anniversary proving particularly popular. In 2022, events around her accession and Coronation were planned for famous homes, opening up the most positive of royal images to tourists and visitors. It's another move towards the modern for the old anniversary celebrations.

One reason for the success of Jubilees has been their ability to adapt while remaining largely the same. The communal feasting and celebrations of George III's anniversary remain but parts that no longer find a resonance have faded away. The more religious society of 1809 was much taken with the notion of remission. A Biblical Jubilee involved forgiveness and a major part of the initial celebrations was an amnesty for deserters as well as a large scale movement to release debtors from jail. This was replicated on a much smaller scale in the Victorian jubilees with deserters again pardoned in 1887, on strict terms, and debtors released across India. But as the twentieth century dawned, that part of the celebrations found less traction and no longer formed part of the imagery of a Jubilee.

Instead, modern technology made Jubilee broadcasts a possibility and they have become a settled part of celebrations since 1935. However, they find their origins in the telegraph sent around the world at the push of a button by Queen Victoria in 1897. Her message was quoted by her grandson, George V, to end his own Silver Jubilee message '*From my heart, I thank my beloved people, may God bless them.*'

In the era of Elizabethan Jubilees, messages have been issued on both Accession day and at the end of the now traditional weekend of celebrations, always with thanks at their very core. The first messages are usually written, the second involve a brief TV statement. But even though those broadcasts last just a few minutes, they bring the Monarchy into millions of homes, reinforcing the positive side of the celebrations. However, the Platinum Jubilee of 2022 brought a new challenge to this now old tradition. The rise of social media meant a constant analysis of royal imagery, never before experienced during a Jubilee.

The Royal Family took to its official accounts with seventy images of the Queen's reign, posting one every day during the final seventy days of the countdown to the long weekend of celebrations. But it was also criticised for not using its channels to do more to defend the Monarchy against criticisms. In a world where younger generations, traditionally less interested in royalty, relied more on social media for news than traditional outlets, it opened a new challenge for the old institution of Jubilees. There was a growing awareness that the Jubilee story was being told more quickly and under more scrutiny that at any time before.

The Queen nodded to that as she hosted a tea party at Sandringham on the eve of the seventieth anniversary of her accession. Invited to cut a cake, she found that its iced representation of her official Jubilee logo was upside down as she looked at it. She was told it was so the photographers could get it the right way up for the pictures that would be seen with millions. *'I don't matter'*, she said before cutting the cake, upside down to its Monarch, with a smile.

The build-up to the first ever Platinum Jubilee also raised the question of holding the celebrations without the star of the show. The Queen's health gave cause for concern in the months ahead of the seventieth anniversary of her accession to the throne. A string of cancelled public engagements led to questions about whether Elizabeth II would be present at the long weekend of festivities. Her appearance at the Service of Thanksgiving for her late husband, the Duke of Edinburgh, held at the end of March 2022 allayed concerns. But the idea of a Jubilee with no Monarch would, in one way, bring the whole celebration back to its very beginnings.

The first ever Jubilee went ahead without anyone catching sight of the Monarch being feted. George III's brief foray outside the walls of the castle where he was convalescing was barely witnessed, but his image was at the heart of parties and parades in his honour around Britain and that was the very point of the Jubilee. The monarch himself was almost surplus to requirements. The celebration of his reign was a reminder of his role in British life which turned him into a figure of unity around which a countrywide festivity arose. But what was ultimately feted were the people creating it. The Jubilee belonged as much to those who marked it as to the Monarch who inspired it.

The same has been true of Jubilees ever since. Each of them has taken on the aspect of the country celebrating them. From the imperial celebration of 1897 when the very notion of nationality was wound up with Empire and the benefits it brought, to the self confident sovereignty of 2012 when Britain boomed, each Jubilee has become a reflection of the people involved.

The actual participation of the Monarch has become expected but, in reality, they are only ever one part of a bigger whole. They are easier to find in the modern world thanks to TV, the internet and newspapers but in 2022, as in 1809, their presence is one part of an image. Jubilees, by their very nature, allow the Monarchy to be seen and believed in.

## Chapter Eleven

# The Platinum Jubilee of Elizabeth II

On the morning of 6 February 2022, Elizabeth II became the only British Monarch to rule for seventy years. She marked the day with an official photo showing her at work on her government boxes and a simple statement which she signed 'Your Servant, Elizabeth R.'

In the hours before, she had hosted a tea party at her Norfolk home, Sandringham, for estate workers and their families as well as members of the local Women's Institute while the run up to this historic day had also seen her photographed reading some of the thousands of cards and letters sent from around the world to mark her many Jubilees. It was a more high profile commemoration of her Accession Day than usual, an acknowledgement of the historic moment which saw her break yet another royal record. But despite the global interest and worldwide headlines, this was just a taster. The main celebrations for the Platinum Jubilee of Elizabeth II were set for the start of June 2022.

The countdown to a four day extravaganza to mark the seventieth anniversary of the Queen's reign started exactly a year before the first party was due to take place. On 2 June 2021, the Royal Family shared plans for a long weekend of Jubilee events. An extra Bank Holiday was confirmed by the UK government to allow time for a string of celebrations. Pomp and pageantry would feature alongside popular parties to mark the Platinum Jubilee of Elizabeth II.

The decision to confirm plans so far in advance came as a surprise. Just weeks earlier, the Queen had sat alone in St. George's Chapel, Windsor for the funeral of her husband of seventy-three years. The death of the Duke of Edinburgh, on 9 April 2021, at the age of ninety-nine had shaken the Royal Family to its core. His widow had mourned in isolation as the Coronavirus pandemic continued to restrict movements. The funeral of her consort was attended by just thirty mourners, in line with government guidelines of the time. Those same restrictions were still easing when the Royal Family announced the main celebrations of the forthcoming Jubilee and questions were raised as to whether such big crowd events would even be possible in a world still dominated by a global pandemic.

But the Queen's eyes were on the future and, not for the first time in her reign, Elizabeth II was ready to tear up the rule book to ensure her Monarchy was seen in its best light. Trooping the Colour, the traditional parade marking the Sovereign's Official Birthday, would be moved from its regular Saturday spot to a Thursday to allow its ceremonial splendour to start the Jubilee celebrations. On 2 June 2022, the Queen would lead a carriage parade of her Royal Family from Buckingham Palace to Horseguards Parade where the 1st Battalion Irish Guards would troop their colour. The Royal Family would then return to the Palace for a flypast and a balcony appearance. A huge turnout was expected and the ballot for tickets was eagerly anticipated, seeing record applications as soon as it opened in February 2022.

The Queen, who would turn ninety-six less than six weeks before this extravaganza, would then rest. The next phase of Jubilee celebrations was planned to take place as darkness fell. On the evening of 2 June 2022, a chain of beacons would be lit up across the UK and around the world and Elizabeth II's beacon would be the most significant of all.

The tradition of lighting emblematic fires for major royal events stretches back centuries and had been an integral part of other British royal jubilees. However, its significance was amplified in Platinum Jubilee year as the beacon lighting became part of a programme turning it into the first community event of a celebration designed around popular participation. Communities were encouraged to take part with either bonfires, torches or, preferably, beacons. Many metal stands from past royal celebrations were still in place but Jubilee organisers developed easy to follow plans for new beacon cases, asking villages and towns to consider getting local crafters to create an artwork from scratch that could become part of their area's history. By the time registration closed, over 3,000 beacons were already listed as ready for lighting for the Platinum Jubilee.

Organisers pinned their hopes of each being heralded into existence with local pomp and ceremony. Town criers were encouraged to dust down their regalia and announce the beacon chain in the hours ahead of the lightings. A special piece of music for pipes, *Diu Regnare*, was composed while a brand new bugle call to be used ahead of the beacons springing into life was created. The very modern nature of this Jubilee was underlined by them being shared on websites via downloads.

A Song for the Jubilee, to be performed as the beacons were lit, was distributed in the same way. It was the result of a competition, a theme throughout the Platinum celebrations which saw many major elements of the festivities decided through contests open to people across the Commonwealth. The race to write a Jubilee song began as the Royal Family was announcing the party plans in June 2021. The winning entry, 'A Life lived with Grace', was ready for uploading to the official celebratory websites within months, with choirs around the world encouraged to learn it in time to sing as the beacons were lit. And all this was just the opening act.

The second day of the Platinum Jubilee weekend would see the Queen and the Royal Family travel to St. Paul's Cathedral for a Service of Thanksgiving for her long reign. While several thousand would join her for a ceremony led by the primates of the Church of England, religious communities around the UK were being encouraged to put their faith groups at the heart of Jubilee celebrations. The Queen has spoken often of her strong Christian beliefs and the emphasis on religion in her Platinum celebrations was noticeable.

Special resources were produced for churches and faith groups to use in ceremonies marking her Jubilee giving thanks for her reign. There was a campaign for communities to commit to 'Seventy Acts of Service' while an anthem, 'Rise Up and Serve', was composed for the occasion for choirs and congregations to sing on Jubilee weekend. The Church of England offered suggestions for special services on the anniversary of the Queen's Accession, 6 February, which fell on a Sunday, as well as for the final day of her Jubilee weekend, Sunday, 5 June 2022 which was also the feast of Pentecost, the Christian festival which had helped boost the notion of Jubilees centuries earlier.

Despite the dominance of Westminster Abbey as a religious setting for major royal events, the choice of St. Paul's Cathedral for the Platinum Jubilee service followed a long tradition. Queen Victoria had been the first British Monarch to mark a Jubilee there when the great and good of her kingdom stood outside for a special service for the sixtieth anniversary of her reign to allow the Queen, by then old and infirm, to join in from her carriage without having to negotiate steps. Her great, great granddaughter had suffered her own mobility issues in the months before her Platinum Jubilee but, despite being almost two decades older than Victoria had been when the church came to her in 1897, Elizabeth II planned to walk into the service where thousands would give thanks for her life and reign in 2022.

It was expected to be another magnet for crowds with thousands set to line the route through central London for a glimpse of the Jubilee Queen. Getting close to Elizabeth II would prove harder at the next showpiece of her celebratory weekend. On 4 June 2022, the Queen's love of horses dominated as her Jubilee plans were built around the Epsom Derby. The famous flat race had been a summer highlight for Elizabeth II throughout her reign and it remains ticket only. Admission for the race, always in high demand, saw some areas including the much coveted Queen's Stand, selling out quickly in 2022. Associated with royalty for much of its long history, its incorporation into the official Jubilee celebrations again, following its role in the 2012 events, cemented its prestige as well as making it one of the hottest tickets of the year. The promise that many of the Royal Family, even those who didn't always share the Queen's love of racing, would be present only increased interest. But one of the biggest draws for this rather commercial part of the celebrations was the possibility of seeing Elizabeth II as a lifelong dream came true.

For decades, the Queen had been one of the most successful and admired horse breeders in the UK but one prize had always eluded her. Despite many great runners and some close calls, she had never won the Derby, the race she really wanted to bag. As 2022 got under way, experts felt that her Platinum Jubilee year might be the time her fortunes changed. Her horse, Reach for the Moon, placed well in a number of runs seen as good indicators for the Derby while commentators began to mention the ever growing chances of a royal win for the Platinum Queen.

She would get little chance to celebrate if she did prove successful. The third day of the Platinum weekend was given over to what had become one of the mainstays of the Elizabethan Jubilee, a 'Party at the Palace'. Just an hour after the Derby winner was confirmed, the Royal Family was expected on the Mall for a huge concert.

The 2002 innovation of a giant musical event at Buckingham Palace had cemented itself in the public consciousness so well that the concept of a Jubilee without one seemed impossible. While the Golden Jubilee had seen both a classical show and a pop concert take over central London, the Platinum celebrations followed the pattern of the Diamond events and stuck to one event only. It promised some of the biggest names in modern music with George Ezra, himself born long after the Silver Jubilee of Elizabeth II, confirmed as the first headline act in early 2022.

Tickets for the event would be distributed by ballot. There was some controversy when it was confirmed that entry would be limited to UK residents only – despite concerns over the pandemic, tens of thousands of people planned to travel from around the world to London for the Jubilee weekend. Demand was so high that applicants could ask for just two entries each. In total, ten thousand people would be invited to the concert although many more were expected to gather in central London to soak up the atmosphere and the music from a distance.

They would be in pole position for the final spectacular planned for the Jubilee weekend. The last day, 5 June 2022, would be dominated by the Platinum Pageant around Buckingham Palace. The show promised to celebrate the reign of Elizabeth II through carnival and music. Over 3,000 people were lined up to take part in the event, described by organisers as a 'living scrapbook' of the Queen's life and times. Vintage cars and motorbikes as well as performers in vintage clothes were to bring every part of her seventy year rule to life, while artists, including giant corgi puppets, prepared to show all aspects of her historic rule. Another Jubilee competition, this time for schoolchildren to design giant scarves that would form a 'River of Hope' during the Pageant, was also launched in early 2022, ahead of the long weekend.

The final day of the June celebrations was also earmarked for another staple of Elizabethan Jubilees, the street party. For the second celebration in a row, the main focus was the Big Jubilee Lunch, designed to put communities at the heart of the parties. The Big Lunch had been launched in 2009 to provide an opportunity for neighbours to come together. In 2012, it had been transformed for the Diamond Jubilee and, ten years on, the same process was repeated as Elizabeth II became the first British Monarch to mark a Platinum Jubilee. But organisers found themselves sharing some things with their counterparts in the Silver Jubilee year, forty-five years earlier. Parties in the street needed permission and there were forms to fill in to ensure that roads were closed in time for June 2022. Local authorities around England reported high levels of interest in holding street parties for Elizabeth II's seventieth anniversary as Queen and they made good use of a new tool for Jubilees to get their message across.

Social media became an integral part of organising the Platinum Jubilee. Although platforms including Twitter and Facebook had been around for the Diamond Jubilee, by 2022 they were a dominant form of information. The use of social media posts by official organisations and the Royal Family meant that the build up to the Jubilee of 2022 was more sustained than any before. Preparations for the Platinum Party began to appear with regularity on platforms like Instagram, Twitter and Facebook. Councils who wanted to chase forms for street parties only needed to tweet out reminders to make sure they'd done their bit in bringing the Jubilee party to life. Social media also allowed organisers to take more control of how Jubilee news was shared. Fresh details of new ways to celebrate this historic anniversary often originated on official social media channels and every post became news for Jubilee hungry media organisations who spread their own versions of the stories in the same way. By 6 February 2022, the seventieth anniversary of the Queen's reign, the hashtag 'Platinum Jubilee' was cemented on major platforms. A week before the June celebrations, it got its own emoji in the shape of a corgi named PJ.

It was used by plenty of people and groups who had switched their icon to the Platinum Jubilee logo. The official emblem had been revealed at the start of August 2021 following another competition, this time run by the Victoria and Albert museum and open to 16 to 25 year olds. In the end, a teenage graphics design student created the emblem for Britain's only ever Platinum Jubilee. Nineteen-years-old Edward Roberts placed the Crown of St. Edward at the heart of his design. The ancient symbol of royalty was traced in a platinum line on a purple background with its famous top represented by a model of the number seventy. It was surrounded by a circle, to imitate a royal seal, and featured the words 'The Queen's Platinum Jubilee 2002' in the font 'Perpetua', chosen for its meaning of 'forever'.

The emblem was issued with no copyright and made available for Jubilee use with no limitation. That caused surprise in a media savvy age but it harked back to a PR tool first used by Queen Victoria at the time of her Diamond Jubilee. Elizabeth II, like Victoria, was ensuring control of the image of the Jubilee. Just as her great, great grandmother had agreed to anyone using the portrait she issued for her Diamond Jubilee for souvenirs and merchandise, as well as adulatory posters, so the Queen permitted anyone to use the Platinum Jubilee emblem for anything to do with her celebration.

While Victoria had to rely on mass distribution of the photo to ensure her Jubilee looked as she intended, Elizabeth II merely had to point her subjects online. The emblem was available to download from the royal website but it came with strict rules. No changes, in particular to the colour which had been matched as closely as possible to the shade of royal purple used on the Robe of Estate worn by the Queen at her Coronation, were permitted. However tempting an Instagram filter might be, this emblem was designed to look the same every time it appeared.

Victoria didn't have the monopoly on photos either. As preparations continued, the Royal Family took again to its official website to share an image of the Queen which was free to use for charities and non profit organisations. It was soon picked up by many groups, appearing in greater numbers as Jubilee preparations picked up pace and ensuring this smiling snap of Elizabeth II, dressed in pink and holding flowers, became a widely known image of the Monarch in her Jubilee year. Once more, control of the royal image rested with the royals themselves.

Official souvenirs and mementoes appeared soon afterwards, following a theme set by the emblem. The Jubilee took its name from the precious metal, platinum, but its matt grey shade was similar to the silver of Elizabeth II's first Jubilee. Instead, this most royal celebration would be represented by that most royal colour, purple.

As the Royal Collection Trust, the department of the Royal Household that looks after the royal treasures and manages the public opening of its residences, launched the first official souvenirs, the emphasis on the link to the Robe of Estate used at the Coronation was highlighted again. The souvenirs were designed in purple with motifs of golden olive leaves and sheafs of wheat, to mimic the robe. There were nods too, to all parts of the UK, with china made in England, tea towels printed in Northern Ireland and souvenir biscuits made in Scotland. Within weeks, commercial enterprises began selling their own Jubilee mementoes. Mugs and plates, biscuit tins and posters began to appear in shops and, distinctive to this Jubilee, online where sales of souvenirs really took hold in the months approaching the celebrations.

Not everyone got it right, though. A wholesaler made headlines in the days before the seventieth anniversary of the Queen's reign when they snapped up a large number of items made in China without a spellchecker. The souvenirs for the 'Jubbly' of Elizabeth II ended up on front pages around the world, on sale as a job lot for £32,000.

By then, money of a much lower value was jangling into pockets with a Jubilee ring about it. The Royal Mint issued a special 50p piece for the seventieth anniversary of Elizabeth II's reign. It was the first time a commemorative 50p had been made for a royal event. It was first released as a special collector's item but on 7 February 2022, the day after the Queen's reign had reached seventy years, it went into general circulation. The coin that hit the tills featured a design by agency Osborne Ross and was personally approved by the Queen. On the reverse side of the coin was the number seventy and inside the zero of this record breaking number were the dates, so far, of Elizabeth II's rule with her Royal Cypher above them. The collector's coin added a further flourish with a specially commissioned portrait of the Queen on horseback created by artist John Bergdahl.

Customers at UK Post Offices were the first to get the coin which went into circulation through their tills. It may well have been handed over as change for purchases of special Jubilee stamps which also went on sale on the same day.

Royal Mail chose to mark the Jubilee with eight different images of the Queen taken across her long reign. Among the photos selected was one of Elizabeth II at her Silver Jubilee of 1977. Alongside images of her at the Order of the Garter ceremony and Trooping the Colour, it was designed to show the many aspects of her historic rule. All eight images were issued as first class stamps and were soon seen on letters being posted across the country. Special collector's editions, including First Day Covers, also went on sale alongside lower value souvenirs including commemorative postcards.

The Royal Mint and the Royal Mail waited until the seventieth anniversary of the Queen's reign itself had been reached before releasing their official Jubilee items. It was accepted practice to only put them into circulation once the event they marked had taken place. However, the Platinum Jubilee of Elizabeth II proved more pressing in that regard for, in the months before reaching seventy years of rule, the Queen had experienced health problems which had given public cause for concern.

Elizabeth II had returned to public duties soon after the death of Prince Philip, hosting a private audience just five days after the Duke of Edinburgh passed away. On 11 May 2021, she had attended the State Opening of Parliament, her first public appearance since her loss. A spate of engagements in early summer had been followed by her traditional summer stay at Balmoral, but on her return to London her pace of public appearances caused comment as she packed events into her diary. Her decision to start using a walking stick also led to debate.

She first appeared with the aid at a service marking the centenary of the Royal British Legion at Westminster Abbey in October 2021 and soon afterwards, made use of it again as she opened a new session of the Welsh Senedd in Cardiff. Buckingham Palace said it was for comfort rather than a specific medical reason. Soon afterwards, the Queen cancelled a string of public engagements including a planned visit to the COP26 summit in Glasgow, sending a video message to world leaders gathered there instead. However, it was her decision to miss the Remembrance Day service at the Cenotaph that caused many to question the extent of her health problems. Leading the nation in remembrance remained vital to her. Royal officials said she had sprained her back but in the weeks that followed, focus on the Queen's health intensified.

The rise of a new strain of Coronavirus, the omicron variant, led to her cancelling further events in December 2021 and scaling back her plans for a family Christmas. In the end, she was joined by the Prince of Wales, the Duchess of Cornwall and the Earl and Countess of Wessex at Windsor on Christmas Day. However, they arrived at St. George's Chapel on 25 December without her. It wasn't clear whether health issues or a security alert, which saw an armed intruder arrested within Castle grounds early in the morning, led to her decision to worship privately that Christmas.

Instead, the only view of Elizabeth II that festive season came in her traditional Christmas Day speech. Dressed in red, and wearing the brooch she had chosen on a honeymoon walk with Prince Philip, she spoke movingly of her loss in her most personal address ever. But amidst her memories and mourning, she had her eye on the future. Touching on her imminent Jubilee, she said she hoped it would 'be an opportunity for people everywhere to enjoy a sense of togetherness' and 'to give thanks for the enormous changes of the last seventy years'. It was clear that whatever issues her health had given her in the past weeks, the Queen was ready for her Jubilee celebrations.

Her royal residences were also preparing to commemorate the milestone. Major exhibitions marking her reign were planned at some of her most high profile homes, while others got ready for popular celebrations that would bring the Platinum party to the heart of Elizabeth II's estate. Buckingham Palace had first opened to the public in the year after the Queen's Ruby Jubilee when, battered by criticism over her family's personal lives and the cost of the Monarchy, the Queen had agreed to the doors of the most famous royal home in the world being thrown open to bring in revenue. The Palace now welcomed paying visitors every summer and for the Platinum Jubilee, the tour would include a special exhibition marking the Queen's Accession.

Iconic early images of Elizabeth II, taken by the ground-breaking photographer Dorothy Wilding who had first been commissioned by King George VI, formed an integral part of the show. And, in a nod to the hugely successful Buckingham Palace show marking the Diamond Jubilee, some of the most famous jewels of Elizabeth II's reign were put on display. Among them was the Girls of Great Britain and Ireland tiara which the Queen had worn for the earliest portraits of her rule including those used on stamps and coins for decades.

Windsor Castle, which had become her regular base in the years before the Platinum Jubilee owing to repairs at Buckingham Palace and its comparative remoteness in the pandemic, celebrated the royal milestone with an exhibition about the Coronation. The Robe of Estate, so vital in informing the colour scheme and image of the Platinum Jubilee, took pride of place in the show. Visitors would get a close view of the golden embroidery of wheat and olive branches, representing prosperity and peace, which had been painstakingly sewn on to it by twelve embroideresses at the Royal School of Needlework almost seven decades before. The robe, created by Ede and Ravenscroft from purple velvet woven by Warner and Sons, stood alongside the famous Coronation dress, designed by Sir Norman Hartnell. The gown featured emblems from all four parts of the United Kingdom as well as floral representations for Commonwealth countries and had become emblematic of the Queen's reign.

Another iconic outfit starred in the exhibition at Holyroodhouse in Edinburgh. The Queen's official home in Scotland showcased her past Jubilees to 2022 visitors with the famous pink coat and dress, designed by Sir Hardy Amies for the Silver celebrations of 1977, one of the most popular displays. Outfits chosen by the Queen for her Golden and Diamond Jubilees also featured.

Less formal royal outfits were the subject of a display at the Queen's Scottish estate at Balmoral where summer visitors were shown what the Monarch chose to wear while pursuing the country walks and sports she is known to enjoy so much. Her celebrated love of animals was at the heart of a show at Sandringham which displayed objects and photos related to her passion for pets and horses. The Norfolk estate also decided to throw open its doors on the first evening of the Jubilee weekend for a special concert by renowned opera singer, Katherine Jenkins, while the final day of the Bank Holiday included a vintage car show.

The Platinum exhibitions at royal estates underlined an ever greater royal determination to set the tone and the tempo of Jubilee celebrations. While organisations like the National Trust, Historic Houses and English Heritage all saw member homes incorporate the Jubilee into summer events in 2022, it was the royal estate that led the way and provided the biggest shows for visitors around the UK. The impact that a good Jubilee could have on image was even examined in one of the exhibitions put on in 2022. Kensington Palace housed a show of hundreds of photographs of royalty for its Jubilee event and openly discussed the importance of a good picture on royal PR with Victoria's 1887 Jubilee portrait featuring amongst its displays.

However, royal focus on the Jubilee wasn't limited to the present. Discussions around events linked to the seventieth anniversary of the reign of Elizabeth II also touched on legacy and one of the biggest projects incorporated a major passion of the House of Windsor. From the earliest days of the Queen's reign, under the guidance of Prince Philip, the royals had made the environment one of their most important issues. The Queen's Green Canopy, to mark the Platinum Jubilee, carried that further. The project aimed to create a new woodland across the UK and the Commonwealth as a lasting tribute to the Queen. Prime Minister Boris Johnson announced the scheme with the catchphrase 'Plant a Tree for the Jubilee' in early 2021 but it was Elizabeth II and her heir, the Prince of Wales, who launched the scheme fully as planting season got under way in the UK.

At the start of October 2021, just before driving to Edinburgh to open a new session of the Scottish Parliament, the Queen went to the Balmoral estate to plant the first of her Jubilee trees. Prince Charles was on hand to help as were local school children who signed up to the project. As cameras clicked, the Queen promised them she would read the handmade booklet about the environment which they gave to her as she made her way to the Scottish capital for her State duties.

Families, schools and community groups as well as big organisations and landowners were all encouraged to get planting to create a canopy of trees to mark the Jubilee. The project was supported by the Woodland Trust which provided free trees to community groups while star names, including Dame Judi Dench, lent their support to it. To keep the Jubilee at the forefront of the scheme, plans were also developed to dedicate a network of seventy ancient woodlands across the UK and to identify seventy ancient trees to mark each year of the Queen's reign.

The focus on green issues also subtly hinted at one of the major changes of Elizabeth II's reign. As she marked its seventieth anniversary, her Royal Family was increasingly turning its attention to big issues rather than strings of individual engagements and princes, princesses, dukes and duchesses were just as likely to be known for their support of special causes as for cutting ribbons or even planting trees. From mental health to supporting victims of domestic abuse, royals had associated themselves ever more closely with issues between the Diamond and Platinum Jubilees.

That shift was seen in one of the first big overseas visits linked to the 2022 celebrations. In February, soon after the seventieth anniversary of the Queen's reign, the Duchess of Cambridge headed to Copenhagen where she was received by Queen Margrethe II who had just marked her own Golden Jubilee. As well as sharing anniversary congratulations, the visit focused on early years education, a long held cause for the duchess who spent time in Denmark learning from local experts and sharing experiences with Crown Princess Mary who had also spent years supporting the issue.

The Jubilee tours which were so vital to the celebration of milestones in Elizabeth II's reign looked very different in 2022. The Queen hadn't travelled overseas since 2015 and the showpiece visits fell to other members of her family. In 2012, she had focused on touring the UK and dispatched younger members of her family to the Commonwealth. The first Platinum Jubilee tours, announced in February 2022, continued that pattern. The Duke and Duchess of Cambridge went to the Caribbean where they visited Belize, the Bahamas and Jamaica in an eight day tour at the end of March. In April, they were followed to the Caribbean by the Earl and Countess of Wessex who visited Antigua and Barbuda, St. Lucia and St. Vincent and the Grenadines soon after the Princess Royal returned from a Jubilee tour of Papua New Guinea.

The Prince of Wales and the Duchess of Cornwall began their Jubilee visits with a three day stay in the Republic of Ireland. It was one of the less high profile visits but ensured that Prince Charles was close to London. The Platinum visits had been announced just days after the Queen tested positive for Covid. Her infection was mild and she made a full recovery although she had to cancel several video engagements during her isolation as her symptoms were troubling her. However, her ill health provided another reminder of the growing importance of the role of her heir who would take on many of the most ceremonial aspects of her Jubilee year.

Among them was the bestowal of city status, a privilege long associated with Jubilees. Since 1977, the Queen had granted the status for her most significant anniversaries. The race to become a Jubilee city in 2022 began several years earlier with towns and local authority areas spending hours debating whether to enter the contest that would lead to the creation of new cities. The Platinum competition was different from its predecessors. In 2002 and 2012, entrants knew that one place in England, Scotland, Wales and Northern Ireland would be chosen at the end of the process. In 2022, the Cabinet Office, which ran the contest, announced that a still to be determined number of areas would be chosen. Furthermore, the contest was opened up to Overseas Territories for the first time and existing cities were also invited to apply for Lord Mayoralty or Lord Provostship status.

In total, thirty-eight places applied for city status. Among them were Gibraltar, Stanley in the Falkland Islands and George Town in the Cayman Islands. Entrants had to showcase their local communities and distinct identities as they worked to prove they were worthy of becoming cities while, in a nod to the celebrations, they were also asked to outline their existing royal links.

The Queen had travelled to previous winning areas to bestow city status but in 2022, it was her heir who did the honours. His first duty, however, was tinged with tragedy. Southend-on-Sea had applied several times before to become a city and had been one of the most high profile contenders as the Platinum Jubilee contest got under way. Each attempt had been led by Southend West MP Sir David Amess, whose passion for creating a city by the sea was well known. However, in October 2021, weeks before the competition closed, he was killed at a constituency surgery. Three days later, the Queen agreed to make Southend a city in his honour. On St. David's Day 2022, the Prince of Wales and the Duchess of Cornwall travelled to the Essex coast to deliver the Letters Patent from the Queen which created the city of Southend and watch as Sir David was, posthumously, made its first freeman. Her quick decision to bestow such an honour in his memory was warmly received and marked one of the most poignant moments of her Jubilee year.

It was far removed from politics but the involvement of ministers in other parts of her Platinum party would prove controversial. Debate about the cost of the Jubilee was markedly quieter than in previous anniversary years but some projects attracted more attention than others. The Department of Education set aside £12 million to produce and provide books about the Jubilee for every schoolchild in the UK leading to questions from some commentators about whether the money should be spent elsewhere. The Queen found herself turned into a subject of political debate in the early months of 2022 as the images of her alone at the Duke of Edinburgh's funeral were widely used by newspapers and online portals in the coverage of 'partygate' which saw Prime Minister Boris Johnson under scrutiny over whether he had broken pandemic rules around that time by joining events held at Downing Street.

The Queen, as always, remained out of political debate but she wasn't afraid to tackle controversial issues. Her message marking her Platinum Jubilee was one of the most eagerly anticipated of her reign and she used it to settle a long standing discussion. Alongside a recommitment to her lifetime promise of service, she said openly that she hoped her daughter-in-law, the Duchess of Cornwall, would be known as Queen Consort when her own reign was over.

The wedding of Camilla Parker Bowles to the Prince of Wales in 2005 had been far from universally popular given the admission that they had had an affair during Charles' first marriage to Diana, Princess of Wales. At the time, it was announced that Camilla would be known as Princess Consort during any reign of her husband to avoid public upset. The Queen was adamant this wasn't enough. Emphasising the vital role played by her own consort, Prince Philip, and her mother, Queen Elizabeth, she declared her wish that Camilla be Queen. One of the angriest debates of her reign ended with a discreet statement that was widely welcomed. Camilla, in turn, thanked the Queen for her 'great honour'.

It would prove to be a bright spot for the Royal Family at a time when its wider reputation was suffering. In the weeks around the seventieth anniversary of her reign, the Queen saw her second son, Prince Andrew, try to stop a civil court case in the US in which he was accused of sexually assaulting a young woman aged seventeen. He always denied the allegations but, in February 2022, agreed to settle out of court for £12 million pounds.

Soon afterwards, the Metropolitan Police said they would investigate claims that the Prince's Foundation, set up by the Prince of Wales, had been involved in offering cash for honours. Prince Charles maintained he had known nothing of the claims which touched on one of his aides, Michael Fawcett. At the same time, Charles' younger son, Prince Harry, took the Home Office to court over its decision not to provide him with Metropolitan Police protection while in the UK following his decision to step back as a senior royal in 2020. Talk of another 'annus horribilis' began just as the Queen prepared to celebrate.

The ongoing rows around members of her family were tabloid fodder. Both Prince Andrew and Prince Harry had been told to stop using their HRH status in public but calls continued for both to lose their dukedoms. There was also debate about whether they should receive a Platinum Jubilee medal. The commemorative honour, designed by Timothy Noad of the College of Arms, was to be distributed to every member of the Royal Family as well as to members of the emergency services and Armed Forces who had served five years or longer. It followed a long tradition of Jubilee medals and Elizabeth II showed no signs of stopping all her descendants being honoured with it.

Instead, the star of the Jubilee carried on as normal. The early months of 2022 saw new events announced to mark her anniversary including a Platinum pudding contest in which cooks from around Britain were asked to come up with a dessert fit for royalty. Top chef and judge, Monica Galetti, later revealed the most popular ingredient in the entries was gin, long reported to be the favourite tipple of the Queen.

Despite the troubles affecting her family and the occasional brush with controversy, the build up to the Platinum Jubilee of Elizabeth II always returned to one issue. More than any other Jubilee of her long reign, this particular party was seen as a thank you to the longest reigning Monarch in British history. In an echo of the apocryphal moment from Victoria's Diamond Jubilee when an enthusiastic Eastender is said to have told her 'you done it well, old girl', the mood as her successor's great anniversary approached was one of congratulations and gratitude. Amidst the debate about whether the House of Windsor could survive without her was a general sense of an unparalleled achievement by a woman who was never meant to rule.

The Queen herself was ever careful to acknowledge the contributions of others to her record breaking reign. She left Windsor Castle two weeks before Jubilee Day to return to Sandringham. There, she spent time at Wood Farm where the Duke of Edinburgh had lived for much of his retirement, a reminder of the man she had acknowledged as her 'strength and stay'. But it also allowed her to mark the seventieth anniversary of her reign in the place where her rule had begun.

Her beloved father, King George VI, had been at the Norfolk estate on 5 February 1952 and, after what was described as a happy family dinner, had retired for the night. He was seen at some point after the clock struck midnight, heralding the start of 6 February. However, when a servant went to wake him later that morning, he was found to have died in his sleep. The exact time of his passing has never been known. His death was confirmed at around 7.30am on 6 February 1952. At some point in the hours before, silently and without witness, his Crown had passed to his daughter, Elizabeth, then thousands of miles away in Kenya on a tour she was undertaking on his behalf.

As the world looked to her as she became the only British Monarch to mark a Platinum Jubilee, George VI was ever present. The official picture marking the seventieth anniversary of her rule showed her with the government boxes he had taught her to work through, while on a nearby table was a photograph of the King. In her statement marking this moment in time, she described the anniversary of her accession as still being, for her, as much about his death as her own rule.

Her written message also spoke of the sacrifices made by Prince Philip to support her and the hard work of her own mother as consort to her father as well as her admiration for Camilla, the consort to come.

In some ways, her own achievement was the least of her concerns. She spoke of her hopes that her Jubilee year would allow people to come together and of her hope that young people, in particular, would enjoy opportunities to progress. But most striking was her renewal of her promise to serve. After months of concern over her health and questions over whether she might be about to abdicate, the Queen had an answer to all who asked, telling them '*it gives me great pleasure to renew to you the pledge I gave in 1947, that my life will always be devoted to your service*.'

As the world prepared to hail her achievements, as some spoke of her reign being not just record breaking but perhaps the greatest Britain had ever known, the Queen's focus was the same. Her final words on Jubilee day were simple, 'Your Servant, Elizabeth R.'

## Chapter Twelve

# The Future of Royal Celebrations

The Platinum Jubilee was much anticipated and, given the Queen's long and healthy life, partly taken for granted. After three huge Jubilees in just two decades, the celebrations had developed a comforting regularity in their rhythm. However, 2022 brought with it a realisation that a new age of Jubilees might be reaching its end point. The Queen herself referred to a change of Monarchs in her Platinum Jubilee message and, unlike previous anniversaries, there was no clear path ahead in 2022 towards a new set of similar celebrations in the future.

Ever since her Golden Jubilee, the Queen had been followed around by a rather unwelcome phrase. 'If she lives as long as her mother' was used to refer to the remarkable longevity of this branch of the House of Windsor. The Queen Mother had been a few months away from her 102nd birthday when she passed away in March 2002. Her elder daughter had shown the same good health and general fortitude as that first Queen Elizabeth of the twentieth century and might well expect to live beyond 100. That would take her past the seventy-fifth anniversary of her reign but no one could possibly expect a centenarian to lead a nation in a weekend long extravaganza to mark that milestone. The Platinum Jubilee brought with it a realisation that a similar event wouldn't come around again any time soon.

The Queen herself was always the first to acknowledge her mortality. In her speech to the COP26 summit in Glasgow, delivered by video in November 2021, she spoke of protecting the environment for future generations, saying 'we none of us will live forever'. Just days later she recorded a message for the General Synod of the

Church of England in which she reminded those listening that 'none of us can slow the passage of time' and as she marked her actual Jubilee, she reminded the world that the future wasn't just about her. In the message released on 6 February 2022, she referred to a reign to come, saying 'when, in the fullness of time, my son Charles becomes King'. Even as she made history, she acknowledged that the image of royalty was moving on.

However, her son had also hinted that his own expectations of a Jubilee were limited. Prince Charles had been just three when his mother took the throne. At the time of the Platinum Jubilee, he was seventy-three and the longest serving heir in British history. He had made no secret of his desire to remain a prince in waiting for as long as possible, saying in a documentary marking his own seventieth birthday 'if I have to succeed' and adding that 'there's only room for one sovereign at a time, not two'. The chances of his reign lasting long enough for a Silver Jubilee were slim. Looking ahead, the most probable setting for a future Jubilee was well into the twenty-first century, as a milestone in the reign of King William V. This alteration to an almost predictable pattern would be a change and challenge for the Monarchy.

The Jubilees of Elizabeth II had provided an unparalleled opportunity to position the Royal Family at the heart of national life. The increasingly elaborate celebrations had become an important part of bolstering the Monarchy's image in the twenty-first century and had arguably helped it recover from some of its biggest crises in modern times including the death of Diana, Princess of Wales. Five years after the Royal Family had seen its popularity evaporate in the anger that followed her sudden loss on 31 August 1997, the Queen had managed to unite the country behind the Royal Family for her Golden celebration. Then, as at other Jubilees, the combination of popular parties, pomp and ceremony and the calm and dutiful attitude of Elizabeth II had been a winning combination that had kept the House of Windsor moving forward.

Jubilees had also come to provide a sense of communal celebration not necessarily found in other royal events. The Queen's Coronation had been hugely popular but had come just eight years after the end of the Second World War. The events of June 1953 had been seen as the start of a new Elizabethan age and a chance for Britain to celebrate as rationing lifted and the hardships of war and its aftermath began to recede. However, the reception at the time of her father's Coronation, in 1937, had been more mixed, coming hot on the heels of the controversy of the Abdication and at a time when unemployment was high and living conditions harsh. In 1911, the crowning of George V had been played out against the backdrop of a constitutional crisis.

Soon after the Queen used her Platinum Jubilee message to endorse the Duchess of Cornwall in due course becoming Queen Consort, attention turned again to the prospect of a Coronation. Prince Charles' plans for his own ceremony, dubbed Operation Golden Orb, appeared in newspapers. The event was set to be shorter and simpler than that provided for his mother. Just as George V had slashed the number of people inside Westminster Abbey for his own Coronation in 1911, allowing around 6,000 to witness the ancient ceremony, so Charles planned to cut numbers to around 2,000 and not every member of the Royal Family could expect an invitation. One of the main motivations was cost with the Prince of Wales fixed on reducing expense, well aware that another spectacular ceremony would be needed for his own heir within a matter of years and there might be limited public appetite to shell out twice in a relatively short period of time for two major royal events.

Instead, the focus for royal celebrations turned to other milestones for the Queen. Her own mother had been the star of several high profile birthday celebrations and, following her death, the Queen had taken on that mantle. In 2006, she had welcomed other octogenarians to a special reception and attended two Services of Thanksgiving, one at Windsor and one in London.

In 2016, she had joined in a string of events to mark her ninetieth birthday in Windsor and another set of celebrations in London. Around her actual birthday, 21 April, she had visited a local post office to thank workers for delivering the thousands of cards sent to her and opened a new bandstand in the Queen Alexandra Gardens. A walkabout in Windsor was followed by the presentation of a three-tier purple and gold cake created by Bake Off's most famous winner, Nadiya Hussein. The tradition of lighting torches for big royal events had continued with the Queen setting the flames on the first of a string of beacons that reached around the UK.

Weeks later, her official birthday was marked with a Service of Thanksgiving at St. Paul's Cathedral and a massive street party on the Mall, organised in part by her eldest grandson, Peter Phillips. The Queen had arrived in an open top car and been driven slowly down the Mall as tens of thousands cheered her. Family dinners, complete with big royal photos, completed the celebrations.

Her 100th birthday would take place in 2026. The template for royal centuries had been set by the Queen Mother who marked her own special day with a series of major events including a Service of Thanksgiving which had been attended by the crowned heads of Europe including King Harald V of Norway and Belgium's King Albert II. The Queen Mother had ridden through large crowds along the Mall in a flower-decked carriage with her grandson, the Prince of Wales, at her side before appearing on the Buckingham Palace balcony with her two daughters. Similar celebrations could be expected for Elizabeth II at 100 but the reality remained that royal birthdays didn't have the same popular appeal as a Jubilee.

Between the Platinum Jubilee and the 100th anniversary of the Queen's birth stood another major milestone. On 28 May 2024, the reign of Elizabeth II would reach 72 years and 111 days, making her the longest ruling Monarch in recorded history. In 2015, she had been reticent to mark another historic moment but had found herself at the heart of a celebration nonetheless.

On 9 September 2015, the Queen became the longest reigning Monarch in British history, overtaking the other Jubilee Queen, Victoria. An engagement in Scotland was planned but as she made her way to Tweedbank from Edinburgh by steam train, she found the verges and banks packed with well-wishers. Elizabeth II spent much of that journey at her train window, waving to those who wanted to catch a glimpse of her as she made history. At Tweedbank, where she formally opened the new Scottish Borders railway, there was a brief reference to the day she made history. The Queen told the crowd that *'inevitably, a long life can pass by many milestones, my own is no exception, but I thank you all and the many others at home and overseas for your touching messages of great kindness.'*

Others were far more excited, with news programmes across the UK leading with the story all day and papers and magazines publishing special editions to mark the history-making Queen. Even as her 2022 Jubilee unfolded, those same publications were already speaking of the Platinum Queen's possible brush with history. However, there was also an understanding that this particular milestone would have none of the national resonance that a Jubilee brought with it. This would be very much about Elizabeth II and her personal reign.

Finding a focus for royal celebrations in the twenty-first century always seemed to revert to the Queen. Her long reign had seen another staple of regal jubilation really come into its own but just as Jubilees seemed in short supply in the years after 2022, so, too did that other reason to dust down the bunting, the royal wedding. It had been the father of the Windsor dynasty, George V, who had started the development of monarchical marriages as a truly public celebration and in the 100 years before the Platinum Jubilee, they had come into their own.

Just after Elizabeth II marked the seventieth anniversary of her reign, the centenary of a ground-breaking royal wedding took place. Her aunt, Princess Mary, had married Henry Lascelles in a day of pomp and ceremony that reset the image of the Royal Family. Until the early twentieth century, royal weddings had taken place in royal chapels with royals making up most of the congregation. However, Mary's marriage was set for Westminster Abbey, the first time the daughter of a Monarch had married at the ancient church in over 600 years.

The First World War was still fresh in people's minds and the Royal Family decided to turn Mary's wedding into a moment of national celebration designed to bring cheer at a time of difficulty with the Windsors at the heart of the party. While past royal brides had made short carriage trips through London to their ceremonies, Princess Mary took a longer route and found herself cheered by thousands as she did so. Inside the Abbey, she took her vows in front of a large congregation before leaving on the arm of her new husband to the strains of the Bridal March from Romeo and Juliet by Gounod. An appearance on the Buckingham Palace balcony followed but the PR side of this wedding went much further than smiling and waving.

Mary's wedding dress was the first to be covered by fashion magazines with Vogue among the publications pouring over it in detail. They found a loud statement of patriotism with the gown, designed by Reville of London, containing silk thread woven in Essex and covered in motifs representing the four parts of the kingdom and many of the dominions of George V's empire. Photographs of the bridal party were widely distributed with the less than smiling bride joined by enigmatic bridesmaids including Lady Elizabeth Bowes-Lyon who, the following year, would take a starring role at another royal wedding.

The decision of Elizabeth to marry Mary's brother, Albert, led to a media frenzy that saw their wedding covered in minute detail. The bride's dress was revealed in magazines before the big day with the design, by Madame Handley-Seymour, described in breathless detail. The *Toledo News Bee* praised it for its 'loveliness' before even seeing it while crediting the bride with the choice of symbolic decorations including thistles for her Scottish heritage. Elizabeth emerged from her parents' house to a wall of photographers and showed her own knack of understanding the public mood. As she entered Westminster Abbey, the bride, who had lost her own brother in the Great War, left her flowers on the Tomb of the Unknown Warrior as a tribute to all those killed in conflict.

These two marriages set the template for Windsor weddings in the decades that followed with popular celebration soon attaching itself to the biggest unions of the royal dynasty. The wedding of the then Princess Elizabeth to the Duke of Edinburgh, in 1947, was billed as a moment for Britain to put aside the dark days of the Second World War with the street parties that had accompanied VE Day springing up again for these royal celebrations. It was also the first to be broadcast on radio while photographers were allowed to capture the bride's arrival and departure.

The marriage of her sister, Princess Margaret, to Antony Armstrong-Jones in 1960, took over London with huge crowds lining the street and millions more watching at home as a royal wedding was televised for the first time. In 1981, and informed by the Silver Jubilee of four years earlier, the marriage of the Prince of Wales and Lady Diana Spencer became one of the biggest national celebrations of the twentieth century. Jubilee traditions, including the lighting of beacons, were woven into the celebrations. The wedding day, 29 July, was declared a bank holiday allowing thousands of street parties to take place. Over 750 million people around the world watched it on TV. The marriage of Prince William to Catherine Middleton, on 29 April 2011, brought millions to London for a now established pattern of events, all accompanied by months of build-up and weeks of analysis by press and broadcasters. It became the opening act in a string of events, including the Diamond Jubilee of 2012 and the birth of their first child and future king, George, in 2013, that boosted the Monarchy's appeal for a new generation.

However, royal weddings, unlike Jubilees, proved to need handling with care. The Queen's eldest grandson, Peter Phillips, found himself courting controversy when he decided to sell photos of his wedding to Autumn Kelly at Windsor in 2008 to *Hello!* magazine. Royal weddings weren't for sale but the deal went ahead, regardless. The decision to broadcast the 2018 marriage of his cousin, Princess Eugenie, to Jack Brooksbank attracted debate. The princess, then ninth in line to the throne, gave televised interviews ahead of her big day while the ceremony and carriage ride through Windsor afterwards was shown on ITV to continued questions over why people would be interested. Her sister, Princess Beatrice, was married in the midst of the Coronavirus pandemic in July 2020. Just a handful of photos were released to the press and even then, the bride found herself moved from many front pages the following day by the Queen's other engagement on 17 July 2020. There was more interest in the knighting of 100-year-old war hero, Captain Tom Moore, for his fund raising of some £32 million for the NHS than there was in this royal wedding.

The lack of interest in the celebrations for lower ranking royals highlights the issue the Royal Family face after the Platinum Jubilee. Any big royal weddings are at least twenty years away with the children of the Duke and Duchess of Cambridge most likely to take starring roles in big regal nuptials. Prince George turns nine in the year his great grandmother marks the seventieth anniversary of her reign while his sister, Princess Charlotte, will be seven and their little brother, Prince Louis, will reach his fourth birthday. None are likely to tie the knot before the middle of the twenty-first century. The royal celebration calendar looks rather thin.

However, the House of Windsor had proved itself adept at putting itself at the heart of national celebrations. Along with its recreation of the royal wedding, it has managed to fill the gaps left by history with other moments of rejoicing where its presence was far from necessary but was made to seem indispensable.

In 1951, King George VI and Queen Elizabeth travelled by open landau from Buckingham Palace to St. Paul's Cathedral for a service marking the official opening of the Festival of Britain. The exhibition, showcasing the country's contribution to global culture in the past and its future aspirations in areas as diverse as science, the arts and industry, had been the brainchild of the Labour minister, Herbert Morrison, who wanted to mark the centenary of the Victorian Great Exhibition with an event to boost post war Britain. It was a government funded and driven initiative which captured the public imagination and saw twenty-seven acres of war damaged London rebuilt into the sparkling South Bank which became home to this new festival.

The Royal Family took centre stage at its unveiling. George VI was followed through central London in a carriage procession involving his whole Royal Family. After the service, in an echo of Queen Victoria's Diamond Jubilee, they stood beneath giant Union flags with military, in their most splendid uniforms, behind them. The King's speech, in which he described the Festival as 'a symbol of Britain's abiding courage and vitality' was followed by another carriage procession while the evening saw the Royal Family, again as a whole, head to the South Bank for the official opening of the Royal Festival Hall. It was a glittering display of tiaras and glamour which put the Windsors at the heart of a moment the nation came together.

They had followed a similar path at the London Olympics three years earlier, showing widespread support for the Games and associating themselves with a time of national pride. By the time the Olympics returned to London in 2012, the Royal Family was ready to embrace the celebrations fully and, as a result, became indelibly linked with one of the great British successes of recent years.

The Queen, as is usual for the Head of State of host nations, agreed to open the Games but the way in which she did it took the world by surprise and ensured London 2012 was remembered as much for Elizabeth II as for its sports stars. The Monarch's decision to play opposite James Bond in a sketch that saw her leave Buckingham Palace and pretend to parachute into the Olympic Stadium not only made headlines, it showed the Queen in a new light to a younger audience and boosted her family as a result. In the weeks that followed, the Royal Family attended dozens of events and handed out medals to sports stars in all disciplines, sealing their role in a spectacle that had united the country in celebration and showed it in a sparkling light to the rest of the world. Coming just weeks after the Diamond Jubilee celebrations, it cemented one of the most spectacular years of the Queen's historic reign.

The chances of the UK hosting another Olympics in the coming years are slim although the House of Windsor's ability to find a way to cement itself in the national mood shouldn't be underestimated. Signs of a new way of spreading the royal message have become more evident in recent years. The Royal Family joined Twitter in 2009. Since then, separate accounts for the Prince of Wales and the Duchess of Cornwall and the Duke and Duchess of Cambridge have been set up. They all have official royal accounts on Instagram as did the Duke and Duchess of Sussex until they stepped back as senior royals in early 2020. And in a tech savvy age, the mood of all those accounts has changed considerably.

Originally established to share intermittent news of royal activities, they are now a well resourced channel of information that is helping to shape the family's modern image. But now, as well as providing carefully chosen images of engagements and access to speeches at a click, they have become a way of integrating royals into everyday life.

When seventeen-year-old Emma Radacanu won a place in the US Open final in September 2021, keen tennis fan the Duchess of Cambridge immediately sent a personal tweet. 'What an incredible achievement', she wrote, adding 'we will all be rooting for you tomorrow' and signed it 'C' just to make sure no one missed the fact that this was a one on one message. It was seen by millions of people but not just on social media. In an age of rolling news, it was picked up by media outlets around the world and added to the endless copy being written about Britain's newest star. The royal backing for the eventual champion was widely known about, even by those not on Twitter.

Social media has also provided an opportunity to shape the Royal Family of the future. In the 1990s and early 2000s, birthday portraits of royals were rare and usually confined to big celebrations. However, in the 2010s that changed. New photos, usually with a message of thanks for good wishes, are now shared for many royal birthdays, again providing media outlets with easy stories that take the family into millions of homes with ease. It all helps to form an image of familiarity that is vital to a strong Monarchy.

However, continuity remains as important as does the Queen's famous maxim of needing to be seen to be believed. Supporters of the Monarchy often cite the revenue it brings in from tourism every year as an argument against removing it. But often the showpiece events, like Jubilees, are held up as the pageantry that brings the pounds to Britain. Without a major royal event to focus attention in the years ahead, the next generation of the Windsors will have to work against seeming too ordinary.

The looming end of a string of Jubilees also raised questions as to whether their star had become too integral to the success of the Royal Family for it to thrive without her. The House of Windsor was 105 years old in the year of Elizabeth II's Platinum Jubilee, meaning that she had ruled for two thirds of its existence. The Queen's popularity only continued to grow as her reign reached ever more historic proportions with an IpsosMori poll taken in early February 2022 showing her easily to be the most liked member of her family. The same survey showed her personal popularity had leapt in just a handful of months. The Duke and Duchess of Cambridge came second and third.

The Queen's long life has seen several Monarchies tumble, including that of Greece, to which her husband had originally belonged. The Platinum Jubilee reflected a sense of gratitude for the Queen's long reign but it also brought questions as to how the House of Windsor would fare in the future. The history of Jubilees shows that they are only truly successful when they celebrate a well loved Monarch. The general warmth towards Elizabeth II in the year of her Platinum Jubilee showed her genuine popularity as well as the way that these royal celebrations had become embedded in the public consciousness over twenty years of regular occurrence.

The modern Monarchy traces its roots back to 1066. In almost 1,000 years, just one Sovereign has reached a Platinum Jubilee. The Queen's celebration of 2022 was billed as the first of its kind but it may turn out to be the only one ever seen in the UK. It is a tribute to Elizabeth II that so many people were willing to mark her remarkable achievement.

# Bibliography

An Account of the Jubilee of George III (1810) by 'The Wife of a Naval Officer'

Arlstein, Walter L., *Queen Victoria's Diamond Jubilee* in *History Vol. 66, No. 4* (1997)

Bradford, Sarah, *Queen Elizabeth II: Her Life in our Times,* London (2012)

Brightlingsea Town Council, *Silver Jubilee Souvenir Brightlingsea,* Brightlingsea (1977)

Capital Transport, *London's Golden Jubilee Buses*, Harrow Weald (2002)

Danbury Parish Council, *Danbury Silver Jubilee Celebrations*, Maldon (1977)

de Guitaut, Caroline, *Diamonds: A Jubilee Celebration,* Royal Collection Trust, London (2011)

Gray, Annie, *The Greedy Queen; Eating with Victoria*, London (2017)

Kelly, Angela, *Dressing The Queen, The Jubilee Wardrobe*, London (2012)

King, Greg, *Twilight of Splendour: The Court of Queen Victoria during her Diamond Jubilee Year*, New Jersey (2007)

Lambert, David *Jubilee-ation! A History of Royal Jubilees in Royal Parks,* Swindon (2012)

Major, Joanne and Murden, Sarah, *A Georgian Heroine: The Intriguing Life of Rachel Charlotte Williams Biggs* (2017)

Ormrod, W.M., *The Personal Religion of Edward III* in *Speculum Vol. 64, no. 4 (1989)*

Preston, Thomas, *Jubilee Jottings: The Jubilee of George III*, London (1885)

Queen Victoria, *Diaries and Journals* (published online in 2012)
The Daily Mirror, *Sixty Glorious Years, Our Queen Elizabeth*, Yeovil (2012)
*The Queen, the Official Platinum Jubilee Souvenir*, London (2022)
Titchmarsh, Alan, *Elizabeth, Her Life, Our Times*, London (2012)
Worsley, Lucy, *Queen Victoria,* London (2018)

# Index